Pulling Wis

Dr. Hung's book is a must-read for medical practitioners everywhere. She masterfully weaves together her personal experiences as an immigrant, her medical expertise, and practical frameworks to offer an extremely practical book to promote better healthcare for everyone. I work with hospitals around the world and I can't wait to recommend this book.

David Livermore, PhD

Thought leader on cultural intelligence and global leadership

I've had both amazing and appalling experiences with doctors, dentists, and healthcare professionals over the course of a lifetime of global travel and know how critical it is to connect with people across cultures. This book is a golden guide to diversity and inclusion awareness and cultural competency. It's a must-read for all healthcare professionals, their supporting staff and suppliers, medical educators, and students.

Deborah Torres Patel

ForbesSpeakers

When Cathy informed me that she was working on a book about cultural communication in the healthcare setting, I knew right away that it was going to be an instant hit. Often, even with the greatest of intentions, we end up offending patients from different cultures, as we don't understand how they perceive our gestures, jokes, and mannerisms. We all can up our cultural acumen, and the topics discussed in this book are a wake-up call! Much needed for progressive dentists.

Kianor Shah, DMD, MBA, DICOI, DIDIA

International speaker and implantologist

Founder of Global Summit Institute

In Pulling Wisdom, *Dr. Cathy Hung shares great insights of her journey coming to the US, learning to assimilate into American culture, and dealing with the challenges of being a minority woman and a woman in a male-dominant specialty, all while surviving and thriving. She knows she brings values and that she is a great contributor to the lives of people around her, to her community, and to her profession. Dr. Hung also outlines strategies and techniques to deal with patients from different cultural backgrounds in a way that will open the heart, calm the anxiety, and invite patients to share experiences with her.*

This book is a gem that should be read and shared by all professionals, especially healthcare professionals, because we are truly involved in our patients' lives, not just in the treatment we perform but also in being a part of the overall, holistic care of our patients. The book also opens dialogues within our professional community to be more caring, accepting, and serving. Congratulations, Dr. Hung, on a job well done of a must-read book, undoubtedly the first of many to follow!

Dr. Emily Letran

International speaker and high-performance coach

Founder and host, Action to Win seminar

Serial entrepreneur and TEDx speaker

A thought-provoking story prompting the reader's inward cultural competency journey told through the eyes of a first-generation immigrant from Taiwan, Pulling Wisdom *is a must-read for all dental/medical healthcare providers who practice in this increasingly diverse country called America.*

Dr. Hung brilliantly describes the critical core of learning and practicing cultural competency as dental/medical care professionals, which is earning trust and creating reassuring relationships with patients.

Cultural competency and sensitivity extend far beyond the dental/medical provider and include all team members in a practice caring for a culturally diverse patient population. Dr. Hung provides methods to educate and create awareness of differing cultures while assisting staff in discovering cultural commonalities to bring cultures closer together.

This book will become an outstanding and trusted reference for working with and caring for diverse cultures as dental/medical care providers navigate the ever-changing population in this country. Dr. Hung brings cultural competency for healthcare providers to life in a realistic and simplified way that exceeds any previous educational attempts.

Jane A. Long, EdD

Manager of Learning, Staff Development, and Talent, American Dental Association

A thought-provoking story prompting the reader's inward cultural competency journey told through the eyes of a first-generation immigrant from Taiwan, Pulling Wisdom *is a must-read for all dental/medical healthcare providers who practice in this increasingly diverse country called America.*

Dr. Hung brilliantly describes the critical core of learning and practicing cultural competency as dental/medical care professionals, which is earning trust and creating reassuring relationships with patients.

Cultural competency and sensitivity extend far beyond the dental/medical provider and include all team members in a practice caring for a culturally diverse patient population. Dr. Hung provides methods to educate and create awareness of differing cultures while assisting staff in discovering cultural commonalities to bring cultures closer together.

This book will become an outstanding and trusted reference for working with and caring for diverse cultures as dental/medical care providers navigate the ever-changing population in this country. Dr. Hung brings cultural competency for healthcare providers to life in a realistic and simplified way that exceeds any previous educational attempts.

Jane A. Long, EdD

Manager of Learning, Staff Development, and Talent, American Dental Association

PULLING
wisdom

DR. CATHY HUNG

萃取智慧

PULLING
wisdom

FILLING THE GAPS
of CROSS-CULTURAL
COMMUNICATION *for*
HEALTHCARE PROVIDERS

Advantage®

Published by Advantage, Charleston, South Carolina.
Member of Advantage Media Group.

ADVANTAGE is a registered trademark, and the Advantage colophon is a trademark of Advantage Media Group, Inc.

Printed in the United States of America.

10 9 8 7 6 5 4 3 2 1

ISBN: 978-1-64225-141-8
LCCN: 2020907176

Book design by Megan Elger.

This publication is designed to provide accurate and authoritative information in regard to the subject matter covered. It is sold with the understanding that the publisher is not engaged in rendering legal, accounting, or other professional services. If legal advice or other expert assistance is required, the services of a competent professional person should be sought.

Advantage Media Group is proud to be a part of the Tree Neutral® program. Tree Neutral offsets the number of trees consumed in the production and printing of this book by taking proactive steps such as planting trees in direct proportion to the number of trees used to print books. To learn more about Tree Neutral, please visit **www.treeneutral.com**.

Advantage Media Group is a publisher of business, self-improvement, and professional development books and online learning. We help entrepreneurs, business leaders, and professionals share their Stories, Passion, and Knowledge to help others Learn & Grow. Do you have a manuscript or book idea that you would like us to consider for publishing? Please visit **advantagefamily.com** or call **1.866.775.1696**.

In fond memory of my father, Ying-Yu "Arthur" Hung (1946–2017).

Your unconditional love, devotion, and relentless hard work

cultivated many around you and blossomed in us.

Contents

PART II: DEVELOPING CULTURAL COMPETENCY

PART III: PULLING WISDOM

Foreword

MAXINE FEINBERG, DDS

PAST PRESIDENT, AMERICAN DENTAL ASSOCIATION

In her book *Pulling Wisdom*, Dr. Cathy Hung outlines a comprehensive approach for both dental and medical practices to understand the need for cultural competency. *Pulling Wisdom* is well thought out and well written, and it includes tools and anecdotes from Dr. Hung's own practice to assist the reader.

Dr. Hung gives a thorough account of how all healthcare providers can become more culturally literate, and it gives the reader greater sensitivity to differences in communication styles as a function of nationality and generational factors that influence our patients' needs.

Pulling Wisdom will help improve patients' acceptance of care and facilitate better outcomes by establishing mutual respect and better comprehension for both the patient and the provider.

Dr. Hung clearly outlines a road map to improve and expand your practice by fully engaging patients from diverse backgrounds. The reader will have greater confidence in addressing the needs of all patients.

This book fills a void in the practice management genre and will enlighten the reader and provide concrete advice that will improve providers' skills in communication and sensitivity to their patients' unique circumstances. It should benefit all members of the health-care team.

I would recommend *Pulling Wisdom* to all healthcare providers—it will be well worth their time.

Acknowledgments

Exactly one year before I was writing these words, there was a voice in my head, saying, "I have stories to tell, and I am ready now."

I was in Florida attending the "Action to Win" symposium of my friend Dr. Emily Letran. There, I was introduced to Dan Kennedy's "Magnetic Marketing." I then attended the Super Conference, where I listened to and met with the most incredible businessmen and entrepreneurs of today, including Steve Forbes, Alan Mulally, and Cordia Harrington, to name a few. I was inspired. A couple of months later, I was invited to the Forbes Speakers Symposium in New York City and had the great fortune to be coached by the best in the industry among a group of distinguished professionals: Rusty Shelton, a senior marketing strategist; Caroline Nuttall, a ForbesBooks vice president for member development; and Deborah Torres Patel, a voice coach with Forbes Speakers. It was truly a humbling, eye-opening, and life-changing experience for me. I am very grateful to my now business coaches, the CEO of Advantage|ForbesBooks, Adam Witty; Lee Milteer of Millionaire Smarts; and everyone from the Advantage|ForbesBooks family for your encouragement and for making the entire process of putting this book together as smooth as possible for me. Thanks to VP of News and Experts, Freda Drake, for being behind me with full support.

Since starting the book, I have grown by leaps and bounds emotionally, intellectually, mentally, and professionally through the guidance, encouragement, and enlightenment of my circle of friends. I believe in being in a room where almost everyone is smarter than myself, in order to continue to learn. I feel humble and grateful.

I am most thankful to my friend Dr. Emily Letran, of "Action to Win," international speaker and high-performance coach, for opening my eyes to different perspectives and a new mindset. Her energy is infectious and her enthusiasm to help others is commendable.

I especially want to express my gratitude to Dr. Maxine Feinberg, past American Dental Association (ADA) president, for supporting me in achieving my current position in the ADA's Institute for Diversity in Leadership (IDL) program, class of 2019-2020. Dr. Feinberg is a trailblazer in dentistry and women's leadership, and a true supporter and mentor of women. Also, many thanks for your support in my pursuit of IDL to my radiology professor from Columbia University, Dr. Steven Singer, now a professor and acting chair of the Department of Diagnostic Sciences at Rutgers University.

Our current ADA president, Dr. Chad Gehani, shared some stories with me when I visited him in ADA's Chicago office. It is important to note that minority candidates are taking more leadership roles, with the key message being that diversity and inclusion are going to continue to be a large part of organized professions for years to come. Thank you, Dr. Gehani, for your support and for letting me reference you.

Within ADA, I would also like to thank Dr. Jane Long, the manager of learning, staff development, and talent, for your leadership teachings, guidance, and support on the topics of cultural competency and communication at the IDL program.

Many thanks to Dr. David Livermore of the Cultural Intelligence Center for being kind and supportive during my book-writing process. I decided to become certified in CQ (cultural intelligence) because I feel that Dr. Livermore's work is current and relevant to everyone in today's society.

Special thanks for Dr. Brittany Bergeron, immediate past president and director of corporate relations of the American Association of Women Dentists, for your enthusiasm and support on this very important topic of cultural competency for healthcare professionals. I am so glad we share the same vision.

Special thanks to Dr. Raghunath Puttaiah, tenured professor of the University of Texas A&M College of Dentistry, and owner and operator of OSHA4Dental, for reviewing my HIPAA chapter and ensuring its accuracy. Your expertise is much valued and appreciated.

Big thanks to Mr. Ron Klein, "Grandfather of Possibilities," and Mrs. Arlene Klein for your generous mentorship and friendship in the past year. You are one of a kind.

I want to thank my colleagues from the social media community: Northwestern professor and ADA spokesperson Dr. Robert Picks, the "Purple Cow Wow" of Pick's Group, for being a positive influence in my life. Many thanks to Dr. Kianor Shah, internationally renowned implantologist and founder of the Global Summit Institute, for believing in me since day one of my journey of writing this book about cultural competency. Also thanks to: Dr. Paul Goodman of Dental Nachos, Dr. Greg Charles and Dr. Mike Dai of Dental Clinical Pearls, Dr. Nathan Ho of Dental WinWin, and Dr. Alan Stern of Better, Richer, Stronger for being supportive along my journey.

Lastly, I want to thank my family, my husband Fortunato and

my two middle schoolers, Marco and Massimo, for putting up with my busy work schedule and time away from home. My boys are my muses. They read all my drafts and critiqued me before anyone else did because I wanted to make sure that this book could be understood by a thirteen-year-old.

My utmost gratitude goes to my late father, Mr. Ying-Yu "Arthur" Hung. He was a self-made boomer with parents who died young and unexpectedly. He supported his siblings and worked up General Electric's corporate ladder by studying numerous business books in English on his own time. He always said he had "only" graduated with a degree from a local technical college in Taiwan. He said to me, "Everyone working under me had at least an MBA degree." During his GE years, Mr. Jack Welsh decided to sponsor my father to obtain an e-MBA from Harvard University. My father was grateful and very proud of that achievement. My father absolutely, unconditionally supported my education and was very open-minded with my choices in schooling, career, and family. He was one rare progressive parent of his days. He would wave his hands and say, "Go ahead and do it, you are on the right track."

I often recall my young and tender years in Taipei when my father would take me to visit bookstores. I had the same love for books as my father. We would hang out in the bookstore for hours. In the later years, when he was receiving his cancer treatments, I used to take him to Memorial Sloan-Kettering Cancer Center in Manhattan about once a month. It was often a full-day venture. During the car ride, he would tell old stories, or we would share some comfortable silence together in a car. We often visited a pho restaurant in Edison, New Jersey, on the way back from the hospital. We would order the "number one"—beef pho soup—along with a plate of spring rolls to share. To this day, I occasionally visit that pho joint, sit at our old table, order a number one and a plate of spring rolls, and eat in silence, in remembrance of him.

About the Author

D r. Cathy Hung is a native of Taipei, Taiwan. She lived in Singapore for two years before coming to the United States on a student visa in 1991 at age eighteen. She earned a bachelor of arts in psychology and minored in music at the University of California, Berkeley, and received her Doctor of Dental Surgery (DDS) from Columbia University. She is a board-certified oral and maxillofacial surgeon with more than fifteen years of clinical experience.

She owns and operates Prospect Oral Surgery Center in Monroe Township, New Jersey, which is a very culturally diverse geographic area with a large number of first-generation immigrants from all over the world. Fluent in both Mandarin Chinese and English, Dr. Hung often conducts bilingual consultations in her practice, helping first and second generations of immigrant families to bridge the gaps in communication. She was an award-winning writer for Singapore Chinese newspapers in her younger days.

Dr. Hung is part of the American Dental Association's Institute for Diversity in Leadership program, class of 2019-2020. She is an advocate of women's leadership in dentistry and surgery, and founded the Morning Glory Women Dentists Network of New Jersey as well as the Facebook group "The Talented Dentists." She enjoys writing posts, blogs, and articles on various practice management and clinical topics. She is a guest writer for the American Dental Association's "New Dentist Now" blog and Dental Practice Success column. She was recently honored with a Lifetime Achievement Award as one of the "World's Top 100 Doctors" by the Global Summit Institute for her work in cultural competency and women's leadership.

Growing up, Dr. Hung was trained as a classical pianist and composer. She has two albums of piano original compositions, *Watercolors* and *Bay Sound*, available on CDbaby.com and iTunes.

Her interests include reading, cooking, and travelling. She especially loves red rocks. One of her favorite destinations is Sedona, Arizona.

The Cultural Journey that Started at a Circus Circus Buffet

The limits of my language are the limits of my world.

~ **Ludwig Wittgenstein**

F or me, 1984 was a very good year. The Summer Olympics were going on. Ronald Reagan was president, and most importantly, I came to the US for the first time to visit my uncle. At that time, I was a sixth grader in Taipei, Taiwan. My uncle had just finished his master's degree at Cal State. My mother thought it was a good time to visit before my uncle started working. We were introduced to my aunt-to-be, who had family in Las Vegas.

My family and I went to Los Angeles first. Everything was brand new and massive compared to home. A scoop of ice cream in a waffle cone cost one dollar, and the scoop was twice as big. As I dug my fingers into a big bucket of KFC's fried chicken and sank my teeth into a juicy, sweet nectarine for the first time, I fell in love. My mother promised, "One day we will send you here to the US to study, and you can have as much nectarine as you want." We went to the supermarket, and I saw mountains of nectarines and peaches. I thought this was the country of my dreams.

We went to Disneyland and tried every ride. I bought two magic bendy pencils, the type that you can make into a knot, with red and blue stars printed on them. I thought, nothing can be more American than this! I have those pencils to this day, never used. I also begged my mother to buy me a Strawberry Shortcake dollhouse at the mall. The dollhouse was a giant strawberry that opened into halves of a two-story house with little rooms, furniture, and people in it.

My family also wanted to visit Las Vegas. My mother thought it would be a good idea to stop by Circus Circus for the kids to experience the arcade and the all-you-can-eat buffet. I had eaten at a buffet many times in my home country before, but those spreads were never as massive as the one in Vegas. I remembered people were blond, tall, and walking fast past me. I didn't know any English at that time. At the buffet line, I was curious and took a little bit of everything: ham and cheese, mac 'n cheese, fried chicken (in my opinion, KFC was superior), hamburgers and hotdogs, honeydew and melon. The aroma of food filled the air, and silverware clinking was interspersed with laughter and chatting in a language that was foreign to me. I tried listening to see if I could understand what was being said, but I didn't know a single word. My eyes popped at seeing people constantly getting up to refill all-you-can-drink fountain soda in giant glasses. There was no concept of a refill in my country.

At one point, everyone in my family got up and disappeared into the crowd to get food, and I was left alone at the table with a half-finished plate of food. I bobbed my head, trying to peek through the crowd like a meerkat, and caught a glimpse of my aunt, who then disappeared. I felt uneasy and a bit nervous. Then a waiter came up to me and said something in English with a smile and a friendly tone. I tried to understand him, but couldn't. There was a pause, then he asked again. I shook my head, and he quickly reached over and took the plate away.

When my mother came back to the table, I was annoyed and complained about not being able to finish my meal because someone took the plate away. "Just go get another plate, because it's all-you-can-eat," my mother said. That time at the buffet, I really filled my plate. I blended into the crowd successfully without having to speak a word to anyone.

Back at the table, I was halfway through that plate when I was left alone again. I placed my knife on the right side of the plate and my fork on the left, table etiquette that I learned in my native country meant "not finished with my meal." A waitress came up and said something to me. This time I nodded—remembering what happened the last time when I shook my head. She reached over to take my plate away anyway. I thought, *There's no way that this is an all-you-can-eat-buffet because I am still hungry since people keep taking my plate away.*

That experience imprinted me with such vivid images that I promised myself I would learn the English language well so that no food would be ever taken away from me. It was then I realized that language was paramount to bridging the gaps between people.

THE VALUE OF CULTURE SHOCK

At age eighteen, I came to the US and began college. I first lived on the West Coast in Fresno, California, which was a rather homogenous area, before transferring to UC Berkeley, where there were a lot of people from different places but still many people from my own culture. I then moved to New York to attend dental school. Since there were so many Asians on the West Coast, there wasn't that much culture shock when I first came to the US. But when I moved to New York, I found a lot of different cultures, many that I knew little or nothing about.

But I learned as I went along. I learned to be comfortable with dealing with different types of cultural settings and meeting people from different cultures. In my Columbia dental school class of about eighty students, there were people of all different cultural heritages: Italian, Greek, Jewish, Irish, Indian, Chinese, Korean, and more. My bench partner was from the Bahamas. Many of us were first-generation immigrants. Within the Chinese first-generation immigrants were people who came from Taiwan, mainland China, and Hong Kong. Many spoke a second language. During my oral surgery residency, we had residents from Middle Eastern countries and Russia, as well as Italians and Asians.

I was largely naive and ignorant about other cultures when I first moved to New York City. But over a span of ten years living in the city, I learned about picking up someone's heritage by their last name; for example, Rodriguez is Hispanic, Goldberg is Jewish, Russo is Italian, and Nguyen is Vietnamese. I learned about the good and bad stereotypes of different races, but I was also fortunate to experience different ethnic food. Living in New York City, you can walk just a few blocks and see an ethnic display of different restaurants, anything you want. Indian, Peruvian, Brazilian, Russian, Persian,

The vast representation of restaurants is a product of the melting pot of America. The coexistence of different cuisines represents the coexistence of people of different cultural heritages and national origins.

Malaysian, Mexican, Vietnamese, Japanese, Italian—you name it. The vast representation of restaurants is a product of the melting pot of America. The coexistence of different cuisines represents the coexistence of people of different cultural heritages and national origins. New friendships are often formed over sharing food. Food brings stories. Stories bind people together.

Moving around to live in different places has allowed me to appreciate people from different national origins and differences in cultural beliefs, and to learn to respect individual differences.

What I also found was that other immigrants—even those from other cultures—were comfortable with me. During my residency in New York, I was in a setting that was heavily Hispanic, with a lot of first-generation immigrants and citizens from the Dominican Republic. Interacting with them, I learned about their cultural differences and how to relate to them. My first job was at a Jewish practice, so I also got to learn quite a bit about Jewish culture.

I now practice in the central New Jersey area, about halfway between New York City and Philadelphia. There are many first-generation immigrants from the Middle East, East Asian countries, and other parts of the world. My husband is also a first-generation immigrant. He is from Serracapriola, a small town in Puglia, Italy, with a population of about 3,800 people. Over the years, communicating with my mother-in-law, Nonna—the sweetest soul, whose English consists solely of the words *okay* and *thank you*—has been accomplished through more than speaking. I've learned several of Nonna's recipes only through hand gestures, smiles, and laughs. I've written down her recipes with notes like "two handfuls of flour, one egg, and a pinch of salt," or "hand squeeze the sliced onions and zucchini until dry." Language, per se, has been less important in our conversations, and yet communication is still possible via other means.

In the years leading up to writing this book, I was actively involved in my father's direct care during his illness. He had metastatic prostate cancer and was treated in Memorial Sloan Kettering Cancer Center in New York City. As a healthcare provider, I found it very challenging to maintain objectivity while discussing his care with his oncologist—I was able to communicate as a colleague but, as a family member, I had to always make sure my father's decisions were made based on his best interests. I had to be more than just a language interpreter; I had to communicate through the cultural differences and the decision-making processes while being an advocate for my father's wishes.

These experiences and more led me to a far better understanding of what it means to be culturally competent.

AWARENESS—THE KEY TO BONDING WITH PATIENTS

Over the years, I have found that the key to connecting and bonding on a deeper level with patients and people is to raise awareness of cultural differences. The more you know as a healthcare provider, the easier it is for patients to feel comfortable with you. And the more you can make them feel comfortable, the higher your success. You don't want to end up losing a patient because you said something that you didn't even know was wrong or offensive or that was simply mistaken as meaning something else entirely.

As you start to develop your awareness, you're going to begin to understand how to get your patients to open up to you, something that can be very difficult to do when treating people from cultures different from your own—even with an interpreter.

That's why I'm writing this book. I want to help other healthcare professionals see beyond cultural stereotypes and raise their cultural competency. That's the way to bridge the gaps in communication between you and your patients and to improve your practice success. By increasing your cultural competency, you will find your patients more receptive and you will be able to more readily develop trust—not only on a professional level but also as a human being.

The information I'm sharing is suitable for healthcare professionals in any practice setting, whether in private practice, a nursing home, a rehab facility, or a hospital. It's particularly informative for healthcare professionals practicing in a culturally diverse area or those who just want to improve their cultural awareness and competency.

In this book, I will discuss problems that are commonly present in cross-cultural communication between providers and patients. I will share with you several of my own concepts about second-language acquisition. I will discuss competency and bias that exists in language interpretation. I will also introduce the Amalgamation Scale as a means to predict and assess potential obstacles based on the cultural and language barriers between provider and patient; depending on the degree of the individual's cultural acquisition, there are various ways to improve communication.

Finally, I've included some information on training for team members to improve successful outcomes within your practice—after all, cultural competency should be a practice-wide effort.

I invite you to join me in my cultural journey to see, via the lens of an immigrant doctor, how to pull WISDOM from other cultures.

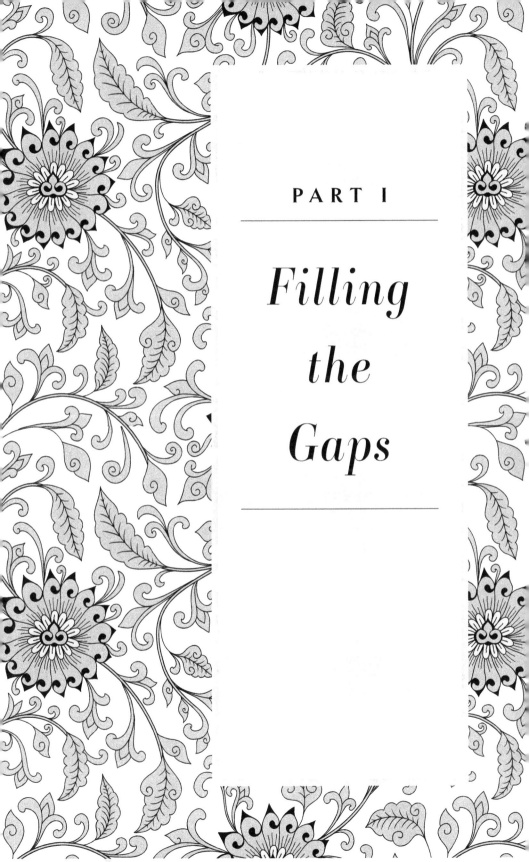

PART I

Filling the Gaps

CHAPTER 1

Muted Aliens

The Perpetual Outsideness of Immigrants

Stereotypes fall in the face of humanity. We human
beings are best understood one at a time.

~ **Anna Quindlen**

When I came to the US as a student, I discovered very early on that there was something I call "the perpetual outsideness of immigrants." It would be two decades before that feeling would change.

Immigrants traveling to the US must apply for a visa depending on the purpose of their visit. When I came to the US in 1991 to go to school, I obtained an F-1 visa, which is classified as a nonimmigrant student visa. An F-1 visa is school-specific and expires at the end of the course study. Over time, I changed schools, and each time I obtained a different F-1 visa for the school where I would study.

During my years of study, I would periodically return home to Taiwan, and each time I had to obtain signatures on my papers from specific school officials prior to traveling. I had to present those signed papers upon re-entry into the US. For ten years, I held F-1 visas. Then, when I began my residency in New York City, I applied for an H-1B visa, which was job-specific and needed to be renewed annually. H-1B visas are issued under a yearly quota, meaning only a certain number of them are granted every year.

During my four years of residency, if I needed to go home or travel abroad, I had to obtain a US visa from a contiguous country, such as Canada or Mexico, before I could travel. The visa to return to the US was not granted automatically just because I had been in the country all that time. Therefore, in order to go home using my Taiwanese passport, I had to first obtain a Canadian visa from the Canadian embassy, then make an appointment with the US embassy to obtain a US visa outside the US. Have I confused you yet? It was a confusing process. I traveled to Canada three times between 2000 and 2004—to Vancouver, Toronto, and Montreal—in order to get my US visa so that I could go home to see my family. In 2003, while going through the visa process, I witnessed two young Muslim women with papers from Boston University being denied US visas, a repercussion of 9/11. After that experience, the fear of not being able to re-enter the country often made me want to jump out of my skin at the US Customs Office—a feeling I recall intensely even to this day.

F-1 and H-1B statuses do not automatically grant you stay in the US after the visas expire. While I was in the US as a "nonimmigrant student" or "nonimmigrant worker," there was never the luxury of taking a break from my course study or pursuit of a job. It was literally either go big or go home.

What struck me while I held those visas was that, all that time, I was what is known as a legal alien. Every time I looked at my documents, even after living here for so long, I was still considered to be an "alien."

What I was feeling is the same thing that a lot of immigrants feel—I was an outsider; I really didn't belong. For a long time, I just felt like I was floating around, like I wasn't really part of America—that perpetual outsideness I mentioned earlier.

Fortunately, when I applied for permanent residency, I was eventually naturalized as a US citizen. That was 2011. After being so accustomed to seeing the word "alien" on my papers for twenty years while living in the US, it was surreal to finally be sworn in and see the word "citizen" in reference to me.

> *What I was feeling is the same thing that a lot of immigrants feel—I was an outsider; I really didn't belong. For a long time, I just felt like I was floating around, like I wasn't really part of America.*

THE NOD OF MISUNDERSTANDING

My reading and test-taking skills were pretty good when I came to the US as a freshman in college. I was on the dean's list for two semesters during the first and second years of my college life at California State University, Fresno. Upon receipt of a letter informing me that I had achieved dean's list, I tossed the letter out, not understanding what that meant.

Still, while my English was improving as I attended school, it took some time to really understand everything that was going on around me in my new environment. That's typical for many immigrants. For instance, when I turned on the television, I didn't quite understand everything that was being said; I didn't know what Brenda was complaining about to Kelly in the original *Beverly Hills, 90210*. As a result, I often shied away from small talk because I didn't know what to talk about. The ease of Americans in carrying on conversations about the weather, food, and what's on TV often amazed me because the concept of small talk doesn't really exist in my culture. I felt muted in social situations; I felt like a muted alien.

Back then, people would often comment, "Oh, you are so quiet." I seemed to fit the female Asian stereotype perfectly—quiet and demure. But it wasn't that I was quiet, I just didn't know English that well. Loss of language somehow dissolved my personality.

My situation was much like that of many non-English-speaking patients, who are often perceived as less intelligent or having hearing issues when they don't respond quickly and colloquially, or verbally at all. When I was in my oral surgery residency, a lot of the patients living in the South Bronx only spoke Spanish. When trying to communicate to a Spanish-speaking patient, one of my coresidents used to speak very loudly, with a grimace, and in exaggerated English to a patient, then add, "Comprende?" at the end of the conversation. We had to remind him, "You know, the patient isn't deaf, he just doesn't speak English." All the while, the patient would nod and smile and just look at us until the end of the speech, then ask, "Qué?"

Taking my own experience back to my practice, I never want to assume a patient's personality as being "quiet" or make comments about it. I prefer to try to ask open-ended questions to gauge their language ability to see if they really understand what is being said. What I have often found with my Mandarin-speaking patients is that they smile and nod when my assistants go over postoperative instructions with them, as though they understand everything that is being said. However, as soon as my assistants are finished going over instructions in English, my patients ask to speak to me, at which point I then reiterate everything in Mandarin. Sometimes I find that only about 10 percent of the instructions are actually understood or retained by the patient. It's likely that at some point you, as a practitioner, may be faced with a blank stare or a nice smile from a patient without them really understanding what has just been explained about the treatment or diagnosis.

Similar challenges are present when paperwork needs to be signed. Many other countries simply don't have as many regulations and consents as the US; many don't even require surgical consent before a body part is removed. When approached to sign various forms about health history, financial information, HIPAA consent, procedure consents, etcetera, many immigrant patients, therefore, tend to be resistant and uneasy about putting names on stacks of papers in a language they are not familiar with. The concept of having to sign new paperwork each time they visit a different doctor is also foreign to them. Understanding basic English terms may already be a challenge, so it's no wonder they may be challenged to understand the medical and legal language on paperwork provided at the doctor's office. The process of learning a second language is nothing like a straight line. Allow me to elaborate further.

THEORY OF SECOND-LANGUAGE ACQUISITION: CHAIN OF ZIGZAGS

Learning and participating in other languages and cultures is a long, gradual process. Reading, writing, comprehension, and speaking the language to eventually learn about the culture, in my own experience, are multiple lines that cross one another at different times only to extend out independently and come back to cross one another again. This learning curve can go on indefinitely. Some people might have more affinity for picking up conversational skills than reading and writing, and vice versa. Ultimately, it is through language that culture is learned.

Based on my own experiences, I have developed a concept to explain this process that I call Second-Language Acquisition: The Chain of Zigzags.

In figure 1.1, reading, writing, comprehension, and speaking are all demonstrated by upward intertwining lines. Each individual zigzag represents the following characteristics:

1. Improvement in any of the areas of language acquisition is not a straight line. There is upward improvement in learning followed by flattening or slowing down during internalization of what's learned.

2. Each of the zigzag lines may overlap one another or multiple zigzags may come together at different points of language acquisition.

3. Some people may possess stronger skills in one area versus another where language acquisition is concerned. For example, some people may be better at picking up conversational skills (such as vendors on the street trying to sell souvenirs to Americans) whereas others may be better at reading or writing skills.

4. There is a general upward trend of the Chain of Zigzags and it may continue to evolve or level off as learning slows down.

5. The chain as a whole represents the culture that accompanies the zigzag lines.

SOMEONE WITH AN URGENT NEED TO IMPROVE ENGLISH PROFICIENCY AS THEIR SECOND LANGUAGE (WORKERS, STUDENTS, ETC.)

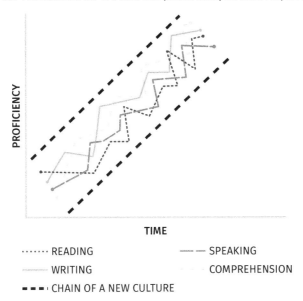

SOMEONE WITHOUT AN URGENT NEED TO IMPROVE ENGLISH PROFICIENCY AS THEIR SECOND LANGUAGE (RETIREES, HOMEMAKERS, ETC.)

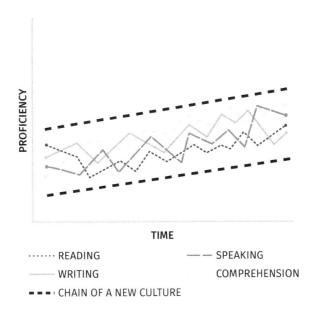

FIGURE 1.1

The Chain of Zigzags can represent one's language-learning process throughout their life. How fast improvement in any particular area happens may have to do with each individual's learning circumstances. For example, someone who comes to the US as a student may improve faster in reading and writing skills instead of in small talk, because it's important to perform well on exams as a student.

> *The Chain of Zigzags can represent one's language-learning process throughout their life. How fast improvement in any particular area happens may have to do with each individual's learning circumstances.*

Understanding the Chain of Zigzags as someone who is actively learning a second language in a different country helps to tame frustration about not being able to "get there" right away. Language acquisition, and finally cultural understanding, is a long, winding road. As a healthcare provider whose first language is English, understanding the Chain of Zigzags will help you to understand why a certain part of communication may come easily while another part of communication may not.

Each person has a different Chain of Zigzags unique to their circumstances. In general, a steeper chain could mean there is a more urgent need to improve the newly acquired second language, the individual acquiring the language has a better innate ability, or a combination. For example, someone who is going through schooling will have a steadier, steeper upward chain compared to someone who may not be going through school or working (figure 1.1). The abilities acquired in four areas of language acquisition, i.e. reading, writing, comprehension, and speaking, may improve at different speeds depending on the setting the individual is in and the immediate need for those particular abilities. For example, my aunt has been working as a florist at Whole Foods Market since she moved to the US; she may not write a twenty-page essay on politics but she is quite gregarious and talks a pretty good sale on flowers in that neighborhood.

Similarly, someone who works as a cashier of a supermarket or a cab driver may quickly improve on conversational skills compared to other areas of skills. An electrical engineer working in a company might improve quickly on the technical part of the language pertaining to the work environment as opposed to other areas. For someone who does not have an urgent need to improve language for school or work, such as a retiree, these skills are not likely to improve a great deal. Their Chain of Zigzags will be flat. My late father, a retired GE executive, used to have TV on all day long playing only Chinese programs simply because he no longer had the urgent need to improve his English.

WHEN ENGLISH IS NOT THE NATIVE TONGUE

An immigrant doctor who comes to this country after their formative years, meaning during or after college, or after professional schooling, may have a very steep Chain of Zigzags because all four aspects of language abilities (reading, writing, comprehension, and speaking) need to be improved within a shorter period of time. The Chain of Zigzags involves improvement followed by a dormant period of internalization before improving again. Utilization of all four skill areas is required to improve the communication skills beyond the basics.

For a healthcare professional whose native tongue is not English, basic skills using simple words, phrases, and sentences are not sufficient to deal with the complexity of the job. The Chain of Zigzags will be a steep one, requiring all four abilities to become polished. Explaining a key concept to your patient, whether it's simple or complicated, requires three steps:

1. understanding the concept yourself (carried over from the already-learned concept in native language or newly acquired concept in second language),

2. internalizing the concept (translating in your mind from your native language to second language), and

3. verbalizing the concept to your patient in the second language (in this case, English).

Reading and comprehension are often more passive processes, whereas speaking requires active involvement and reaction time, which varies depending on the language proficiency one has. When I was in my surgical residency, I often found it challenging to be put on the spot, or to be "pimped," when being asked questions during daily rounds, grand rounds, or Journal Club, because the passive information I read from books needed to be spliced, rearranged, and organized into my own words as quick responses. The "switch" between the two languages wasn't natural, and much practice was needed. The term "pimping" in a medical context was coined by Dr. Frederick Brancati in his 1989 article "The Art of Pimping" in the *Journal of the American Medical Association*. The ability to shoot out answers in response to unpredictable questions is necessarily developed in medical and surgical residency. The inability to answer such questions often causes public embarrassment and scolding by attending physicians and surgeons. Techniques are developed to memorize quick facts, often in the form of mnemonics, and one might seem smarter than another if they already have the skills mastered during rounds. But it was always difficult for me during my residency, as my English proficiency was not completely developed at that time. My Chain of Zigzags was steep in the areas of reading and comprehension, but less so in writing and even less in speaking. These skills do not improve at the same speed. Presentations required much preparation for me to develop confidence and proficiency. The ability to memorize and then recall information in a second language often lags behind the ability to read and comprehend.

Using the Chain of Zigzags in your daily practice can help you learn to pick up cues from patients as to which area of the language patients may have trouble with, in order to mend the gaps in your communication. Do they need help to fill out patient forms? Are you using a word that is too difficult? Ask open-ended questions. Avoid assumptions or stereotypes, and ask for help from qualified individuals.

IMPROVE YOUR
Cultural Competency

1. When a non-English-speaking patient is being quiet and agreeable, do not assume that this behavior is a product of their personality.

2. Ask open-ended questions to find out if a patient understands your inquiry instead of using only closed-ended, yes/no questions. A patient may understand certain parts of your conversation but not others.

3. The second-language acquisition process can be explained

by the Chain of Zigzags. All four skills—reading, writing, comprehension, and speaking—improve at different speeds.

4. Each person's Chain of Zigzags is unique based on the learning circumstances.

5. Understanding the process of second-language acquisition helps us to mend the communication gaps.

CHAPTER 2

The Dichotomy of Treatment Trust

A physician is obligated to consider more than
a diseased organ, more even than the whole
man—he must view the man in his world.

~ **Dr. Harvey Cushing**

My father was diagnosed with prostate cancer in December 2005. He underwent radical prostatectomy at the University of Chicago Medical Center and subsequently initiated standard hormonal injection treatment at Memorial Sloan Kettering Cancer Center in New York City. He remained stable for five or six years before the treatment became ineffective, at which point it was suggested that he enter a clinical trial.

Before the trial, my father was given consent forms to sign. The forms stated the risks, benefits, and alternatives along with side effects of each drug. Luckily, his treatments had been uneventful up to that point; he was satisfied with his care and trusted the doctors at the cancer center. I remember him showing me insurance statements that listed how much of his copays were picked up by the hospital and how much of a financial burden was lifted off of him. He was forever grateful because, as a retiree, he was on a limited income.

The first clinical trial he entered lasted three years before it became ineffective. His prostate-specific antigen (PSA) level was rising and we started to see metastasis in his right femur along with other sites. He received radiation therapy to his right femur, after which he was offered the second clinical trial. He gladly signed up for it, but this time I was concerned.

There was a significant difference between the first and the second clinical trials. The first trial was a combination regimen of two FDA-approved drugs—enzalutamide and abiraterone—plus prednisone. Overall, my father tolerated them well, despite occasional leg pain and decreased appetite. The second trial's drug had a name that sounded like a futuristic robot, a combination of letters and numbers. That meant it was a drug that was not yet FDA approved.

I cringed at the thought of my father taking an experimental drug, but he was optimistic. He trusted the doctor and the hospital, both of which had removed thousands of dollars from his hospital bill, provided quality service, and extended his lifespan so that he got to spend his last years enjoying his grandsons.

Two weeks after starting the trial, I received a phone call from my mother around five thirty in the morning. She panicked and told me that my father was falling in and out of consciousness. I rushed over and found him lying in bed, hunching over a wastebasket, retching and vomiting coffee ground-like blood clots. He was pale, clammy, and sweating, and his legs were swollen to the size of an elephant's. I took his blood pressure: it was 220/100. I called for an ambulance, and he was transported to the hospital.

After my father was stabilized in the emergency room, the healthcare team reported his condition to me: his glucose level was nearly three hundred. Hyperglycemia, or high blood sugar, was a listed potential side effect of the drug, as was hypertension, or high blood pressure.

His condition made me angry and a little hopeless. On the inside, I wanted to scream at the top of my lungs and tell everyone off. I felt exhausted by the early-morning emergency and dealing with my father's life-threatening condition.

But the professional in me took over. I texted his oncologist, then we spoke on the phone. Even though I was upset as a family member, in the call I kept my composure as a professional. I sent over screenshots of the bloodwork taken in the emergency room, and we discussed my father's situation as medical professionals would, exchanging notes. He addressed me as a doctor, and we both agreed that we should stop the trial medications immediately.

I told my dad that I spoke with the doctor and that we would stop the trial, leaving only one other option for his treatment: chemotherapy.

My father nodded. He didn't protest, nor was he angry. He was spent and wanted to go home.

While dealing with his illness, in his heart he had accepted that the best treatment options were offered to him. But he also felt that he owed it to the oncologist to go through with the trial because his medical expenses were paid by the hospital. He felt that he was "returning a favor" by being a subject in the trial.

My father was a baby boomer, born in the southern part of Taiwan during the post-Japanese colonial era. At that time, doctors were treated with the utmost respect. There was no questioning of a doctor's credentials or decisions. If my father disagreed with a doctor in his heart, he would simply walk away without protesting.

In this case, my father received years of treatment that had proven to be successful and that bought him extra years of life. He accepted the doctor's treatment without question even though the trial drug could prove to be harmful to him, as it did.

What my father experienced is a fairly common phenomenon in many Asian cultures, but can certainly be present other cultures as well. It's what I called the Dichotomy of Treatment Trust: the dichotomy between the overacceptance and autorejection of treatment. I had observed this phenomenon within my own culture. I've also observed this phenomenon within East Asian cultures, some Southeast Asian cultures, and sometimes even certain Middle Eastern cultures.

When I meet a new patient for the first time, I conduct an initial consultation. Most patients who come through my practice, regardless of cultural origin or nationality, go through the consultation in the following steps: we review their medical history together, and patients express their own concerns, asking questions about the procedure, potential recovery time, and how their insurance benefits work. For the most part, the consultation is pretty standard across the board.

However, when I conduct my consultations in Mandarin Chinese, my firsthand interaction with the patient is often *unfiltered* because my patients can gauge from my language ability that we share core cultural beliefs and that I understand them fully in *our* native tongue. Therefore, patients often communicate with me with little or no American context, as opposed to how they would with an English-speaking provider. These Chinese-speaking patients are therefore more open to communicating with me about their real concerns. Surely, this could apply to any first-generation doctor of first-generation patients of the same language and cultural origin. I have encountered many patients of my cultural origin who exhibit overacceptance or autorejection of treatment, based on cultural behavior. Let me elaborate.

OVERACCEPTANCE OF TREATMENT: "YOU ARE THE DOCTOR, I TRUST YOU"

Overacceptance is a relatively common phenomenon, especially in Asian cultures. Overacceptance is an attitude of being completely agreeable to treatment, often for reasons that go beyond simply believing that it's a good option. It is blind trust. It's seen in one of those patients who come in and say to you, "You are the doctor, I trust you. I know you will take care of me." They look at you with gratitude in their eyes, a smile, and may even bow to you. Overacceptance makes a patient perfect in a doctor's eyes; after all, it's easy to treat patients when they smile and readily agree to any treatment offered.

That's what made my father the ideal patient: he was agreeable, pleasant, an easy patient. Similarly, he would often underreport his symptoms, not wanting the doctor to worry. He often reported a pain level of two out of ten when he actually was a five out of ten, and he would even take pain medication the day prior to the doctor's appointment so that his symptoms wouldn't seem as severe and be noticeable enough to report.

The problem is that it is easy to overlook problems with the perfect patient who never complains and is always pleasant. Imagine the same situation happening with a patient in an assisted living facility or nursing home. These patients may have other medical issues, such as dementia or a history of stroke causing impaired speech. Those issues can make them poor historians of their own health and cause them to sometimes be easily dismissed. These patients are the exceptions: they may not be actually agreeable, but because of their impaired ability to communicate, they may be mistaken as being agreeable to treatment. As a provider, it is important to differentiate between overacceptance of treatment due to cultural beliefs and impaired ability to express true intentions.

Whenever I have patients that I would categorize as being similar to my father, I go the extra mile to make sure that they really under-stand the worst-case scenario. After I explain the treatment in detail, I ask if they have any further questions. I often seek feedback from family members who may also act as interpreters.

> *As a provider, it is important to differenti-ate between overac-ceptance of treatment due to cultural beliefs and impaired ability to express true intentions.*

I once treated a wheelchair-bound Filipino patient who had suffered a stroke and lost most of his speech function. He was only able to answer yes or no, but he had the most loving and supportive family imaginable, and I mainly relied on feedback from family members to get a sense of his overall well-being. They spoke a mix of Tagalog and English.

The patient needed to have all his remaining teeth removed, so I allowed his wife and other family members to stay in the room during the procedure, and I asked him to just signal to me yes or no about if he was feeling any discomfort as I worked on him. We kept his appointment short, took frequent stops to check with him, and encouraged the family to ask us questions. They were all very agreeable, much like my father, so I asked additional questions to ensure that the patient was doing okay.

On subsequent visits, I also asked a lot of questions of the family members. For instance, I asked:

- How was the bleeding after the procedure?

- How was the pain after the procedure? Did he have to take pain medications?

- What kind of food was he eating? (The patient was instructed to stay on a purée diet.)

- Did he have any problems swallowing his food? Any choking?

- Do you think we could schedule another visit like last time?

- Do you have any questions for me?

On the first visit following the extraction of his teeth, I thanked the patient's son for helping to transport his father to my operating chair. I thanked him for being a very good son of the family, which was a great compliment for an Asian person helping their parents. The compliments were well received by the family. We bowed slightly to one another as we said goodbye.

After examining the patient, I told him and his family members that everything had gone well since the last visit and we should expect the same for the following visits.

Over time, and because of my attentiveness to not only the patient but also his family, they have become more and more comfortable with me, which has made communication much easier in subsequent visits. In following visits, this patient's wife would always tell me that he didn't have any discomfort after the procedure; he had almost no pain and the healing had gone quickly. She told me this while asking for the patient's confirmation as he nodded and gave me a facial grimace, which was the best he could do in the way of a smile. There were several visits because although removing all of his teeth could have been performed in one visit in an otherwise healthy patient, his medical comorbidity meant that he could not tolerate long procedures. I did a small part of the treatment plan each time and saw him several times until the treatment was completed, which took several months. Although it was cumbersome for the patient and the patient's family to try to coordinate everyone's schedules and transport the patient, this patient went from sweating in fear to calm and comfortable as we completed the last treatment—all because we were able to develop trust.

In addition to overacceptance of treatment, there is an almost polar opposite when treating patients, which is also based on culture: autorejection of treatment.

AUTOREJECTION OF TREATMENT

A couple of years ago, I had a patient who was an immigrant from China who came to me for a growth in her mouth that turned out to be a tumor. She needed surgical treatment. However, in spite of our long discussion about the treatment, she told me that she would be more comfortable flying back to check with her herbal doctor in China before making a decision. I spoke with her in Mandarin, letting her know that I had also grown up with herbal medicine, but that her lesion would need surgical removal as the definitive treatment. It wouldn't simply shrink from taking herbal medicine, as she believed it would. She worked a nice job and was well-spoken and well educated. Health insurance coverage was not an issue. However, the cultural belief that herbal medicine provided another way out was so deeply ingrained in her that she automatically rejected my recommendations.

Many years ago, a gentleman from China came to me for an evaluation of his tongue. This man was in his seventies. He was well-spoken and polite. He was a scholar in China and a book author. He told me that he survived the cultural revolution and escaped from inner Mongolia to the US. He was never a smoker, nor did he drink alcohol, but he had a "canker sore" on his tongue for a long time. What he told me, along with the mouth sore's appearance, made me immediately suspect that the lesion was most likely malignant. I did a biopsy on him, and, sure enough, it was cancer. I told him that I needed to refer him to a head and neck surgeon for further treatment, because he would not only need surgery for this tongue but also additional surgeries, such as neck dissection, and potentially adjunct treatment, such as radiation therapy. He immediately refused my suggestions. He asked me to remove as much of his tongue as I needed to and let the rest be. He told me that he had survived the cultural revolution, lived his life, and was content as things were. He didn't want to have any surgery on his tongue. He then quoted this ancient Chinese sentence to me: "The body, hair, and skin, all have been received from the parents, and so one doesn't dare damage them—that is the beginning of *xiao*."

This quote is a famous reference from *Xiao Jing*, or *The Classics of Filial Piety*, a very important collection of dialogues between scholars representing Confucian philosophy. The concept of filial piety toward parents in Chinese culture is a mixture of respect, obedience, love, and reciprocation from children. In Chinese culture, it is deeply believed that one's physical body derives from parents and therefore we should try to preserve our physical body without removal or violation of body parts, as mutilation of one's body parts infers mutilation to the parents, and therefore disrespect. Typically, body piercing other than ear piercing is frowned upon in my culture for this reason.

When he said that to me, I immediately understood where he was coming from. However, I had to inform him that the proper referral to a head and neck surgeon and additional workup to prep for additional treatment was the standard of care. While I understood the philosophy, it was in his best interest to seek surgical treatment. I told him it was important that he stay alive for his loved ones.

It took some convincing for him to receive care. Each time he saw me, he would ask if I could just remove his tongue cancer on the spot. I told him that was out of my scope and that he needed to seek definitive treatment from the cancer institute. Eventually, he did listen to me and sought treatment. Soon after, however, he and his family moved to the West Coast, and that was the last I heard from him.

In the book *The Good Immigrant*, Priya Minhas tells her story of "How Not to Be" as an immigrant daughter from India. She describes it best: "The need to preserve and nurture all that was left of home was strengthened by the ever-present threat of having everything taken away" and "protecting these traditions was an act of self-preservation."[1] When working with patients from other cultures, it is not uncommon to face resistance when proposing medical or dental treatments that deviate from what the patient was accustomed to back home.

Singh et al., in the 2013 article "Dental Health Attitude in Indian Society," raised concerns and identified factors such as general beliefs around pain, fear, nonavailability of oral health services, lack of education, and tobacco use as current problems in Indian society. The article stated: "This delay in proper care results in added morbidity to the patient, which in turn leads to added costs and which again continues the vicious cycle of the perception that the treatment is expensive." The authors talked about the mentality of "at least trying herbal or local products once" and the patient's intention to "get away with the problem after eating medicines." The authors also felt that there is an "unbridgeable gap" between past Indian medicine and modern Western medicine.[2]

---

1   Priya Minhas, "How Not to Be," in *The Good Immigrant: 26 Writers Reflect on America*, eds. Nikesh Shula and Chinese Suleyman (New York: Little, Brown and Company/The Hachette Group, 2019).

2   P. Singh, A. Bey, and N.D. Gupta, "Dental Health Attitude in Indian Society,"

For example, when a patient presents with a severely decayed impacted wisdom tooth, he or she may refuse to have the tooth removed because "it doesn't hurt" or "but I will end up with fewer teeth." The belief that "it will go away on its own as it did in the past" is hard to sway. A discussion can soon escalate into a debate to avoid the procedure. This patient may be interpreted by the provider as "difficult" or "stubborn." As a provider, this type of patient may need more convincing, especially if the consequences of nontreatment may be detrimental.

The conversation may go something like this:

PROVIDER: *You have a decayed wisdom tooth that is impacted and should come out.*

PATIENT: *But I have no pain. It was hurting me last month, but I am okay now.*

PROVIDER: *The decay will only get worse, and it can become infected.*

PATIENT: *I took some ibuprofen. Do we need to take this tooth out?*

PROVIDER: *Yes. This tooth has no function, and the tooth decay will only get worse.*

PATIENT: *Can I wait another two months? I have to work/ my family is visiting/I don't have pain right now.*

PROVIDER: *I would suggest you don't wait too long. This tooth will become more problematic over time.*

PATIENT: *But I will have less teeth, how do I chew?*

Journal of International Society of Preventive and Community Dentistry 3, no. 2 (2013): 81–84.

PROVIDER: *This tooth is not functional. You are not using this tooth to chew. It's embedded in the jaw.*

PATIENT: *But I have no pain now. I am going home next month. I will ask my doctor there.*

As you can see, a typical conversation becomes circular and frustrating, and almost a badgering process until the provider eventually gives up.

In situations like this, I am typically very open with the patient and discuss the nontreatment scenario. I encourage them to seek second or third opinions from other credible professionals, and those recommendations should be based on the standard of care—they should fall within the limits of care that another licensed professional would offer. I encourage the patient to gather all the information they can, but also inform them that treatment is necessary and that delay may cause the treatment to be more challenging down the line.

It's important to respect the patient's natural affinity to seek care from back home, but also discuss the ease or difficulty of post-op care and long-term follow-up should they decide to go ahead and have the procedure done abroad in their home country. If exchange of documents with a provider in another country becomes necessary, then I take extra measures to ensure that the medical record from abroad is translated properly. That may include required notarization by a certified language interpreter.

Sometimes, even after providing the patient with as much knowledge and resources as possible, they may still refuse treatment. As providers, it is imperative to let the patients know that you are there for them should they change their mind. It is not a bad idea to add: "You know, what I am telling you may be something new to you. I would suggest that you sit on this idea and discuss it with your family. We are professionals and we are here to help. In my opinion, this treatment will serve you best in the long run."

THE TRUTH OF "SAVING FACE"

One phrase that can be difficult to overcome is "I'll think about it." That's because, in many cultures, "I'll think about it" typically means "no." In the Chinese culture, turning someone down is a matter of "saving face." It's about turning them down gently so that you don't hurt their feelings or embarrass them in public. By saying "maybe" or "I'll think about it" instead of "no," you "save" someone's face. In context, the term "face" is synonymous with "ego" or "front." By saving someone's face, you avoid hurting their ego or tearing down their front. This is a very important part of social etiquette in many Asian cultures.

Therefore, don't be surprised if your Asian patient seems agreeable to scheduling the treatment with you, but cancels at a later date. (I am guilty of this myself.) You, as a practitioner, may not always know the real reason for the cancellation. You might hear them say, "I've been too busy lately," or "I'll think about it." The deterring factors could very well be copay, conflicts in philosophy or cultural beliefs, or simply that one of your team members or you did not approach the patient in the right way to make him or her feel comfortable.

One time, I received a direct complaint from an upset mom who brought her daughter in for wisdom teeth consultation. The patient's mother was from China. She complained that my front desk receptionist discussed the copay amount in front of her daughter to embarrass her. My front desk team member did not understand the grounds for the complaint and just thought she was difficult. Although it was a relatively uncommon complaint, this patient's mom did not want to appear as if she couldn't afford the copay in front of her daughter, nor did she want her daughter to know how she would take care of the payment. My front desk team member didn't understand the concept of saving face. After the incident, I instructed my staff to discuss copay in a more discreet manner, especially if the financially responsible party was not the patient.

> *In addition to different cultural beliefs, our communication styles vary across cultures. Are we cramping one another's styles?*

By now, I am sure you can grasp that how we communicate largely depends on our cultural beliefs. In addition to different cultural beliefs, our communication styles vary across cultures. Are we cramping one another's styles? Misunderstandings and conflicts may arise when communication styles are different.

DIRECT VERSUS INDIRECT COMMUNICATION— IT'S A CULTURAL THING

As one might imagine, clashes exist when providers and patients come from different cultural contexts. In some cultures, communication is direct, while in others it's indirect. David Livermore, in his book *Leading with Cultural Intelligence*, talks about low-context (direct communication) versus high-context (indirect communication) cultures. For example, a provider who comes from a culture of low context, such as a German doctor who is very factual and direct in delivering messages, may have trouble reading between the lines when speaking to a Korean patient who comes from a high-context culture. The direct and forward manner of a German doctor may come across as offensive to the Korean patient. Of course, this example may oversimplify a complex picture, because behaviors are also largely influenced by other factors, such as socioeconomic level, education, personality, and so on. But you get the drift.

I used to work in a Jewish practice. When the staff members learned about my father's sickness, they often inquired keenly. I was somewhat uncomfortable talking about the subject openly, because in my culture, we don't typically discuss family members' sicknesses unless it's with close family or friends. Neither sickness nor death is typically discussed in social settings with acquaintances. Knowing that my coworkers meant well, I shared what I felt was appropriate without sounding cold or standoffish to them.

IMPROVE YOUR
Cultural Competency

1. Many patients in Asian cultures may either accept treatment blindly based on their trust in the doctor or reject treatment based on different cultural values. This is what I call the Dichotomy of Treatment Trust. When patients accept treatment too readily, it is important for providers to ask more questions to ensure patients understand all risks and alternatives.

2. When patients automatically reject treatment, find out whether their cultural beliefs play a factor. If so, it's important to openly discuss alternatives. Encourage patients to seek a second opinion but inform the patient of the consequences of delaying treatment.

3. Communication styles are different across cultures. Differences in communication styles can create roadblocks. Speaking too directly to Asians may be interpreted as being harsh.

CHAPTER 3

Bias and Competency of the Interpreters

All language is but a poor translation.

~ **Franz Kafka**

There's a phrase in Cantonese that translates literally as *chicken talking to ducks,* which refers to two people talking in different languages, figuratively or literally. Someone who understands both clucks and quacks is as invaluable as rain in a desert in times of need.

When it comes to working with patients from other cultures, an interpreter can be one of the most valuable tools a healthcare professional has.

During my oral surgery residency in New York's South Bronx, a large number of patients only spoke Spanish. People asked me, "Habla español?" at least ten times a day. There were several Spanish-speaking assistants in the oral surgery clinic who were capable of not only translating the language but facilitating the transfer of crucial information. They took active roles in not just explaining the words but understanding the intricacy of the questions being posed to them. It was such a blessing to be able to simply instruct the assistant to go over post-op instructions with the patient knowing that the entire speech would be delivered confidently and with minimal to no errors. For healthcare professionals, the relief of having trusted assistants, front desk, or nursing staff members as interpreters translates into better overall communication because the interpreter is well-versed in medical language.

Claudia Angelelli, in her book *Medical Interpreting and Cross-Cultural Communication*, discusses the concept of "The Visible Interpreter." The model presents "interpreters who are capable of actively and consciously managing those issues as the interpretation unfolds," and maintains that interpreters "make sure not just of interpersonal and sociopolitical skills but also of the linguistic and psycholinguistic skills."[3]

The interpreter's active role in relaying information between the provider and the patient is not just merely language decoding.

As you can see, the interpreter's active role in relaying information between the provider and the patient is not just merely language decoding. Depending on the interpreter's own experience and knowledge of the subject being relayed, the translated content may vary. One could imagine that the translated content might be different if the interpreter is fluent in the language but has little medical knowledge compared that of a professional interpreter or a medical staff member. One's affect may vary as well. You can imagine that a

---

3   Claudia Angelelli, *Medical Interpreting and Cross-Cultural Communication* (Cambridge: Cambridge University Press, 2004).

professional interpreter's affect would most likely be more neutral, as it was trained to be.

OBJECTIVITY IS KEY

As long as there's a third party involved, translated content may never be precise. Still, we should trust that professional translation and interpretation services can offer more objectivity in general, whether via phone or video.

One exception I encountered was a time when I performed an independent medical examination in Jersey City for an automobile accident claim. Two middle-aged Korean men of similar age came in, one of whom identified himself as a certified interpreter from an independent agency. During the exam, the interpreter stumbled a few times as I asked him to translate basic information, such as health history. He also had some trouble finding words to describe the accident to me. During and after the exam, this interpreter asked me what I thought the "verdict" might be. I made it clear that such discussion was not permissible for this type of exam. I was surprised that, as a certified interpreter, this man would ask such a question. He then went into a long discussion with the claimant in Korean, with tones of surprise and disapproval. I felt that I was under their scrutiny. I questioned the objectivity of this particular interpreter. Most of the professional interpreters I have encountered keep the discussion to a minimum. With an independent medical exam, it is especially important to minimize any discussion between parties. But what I saw in this particular instance was an interaction typically exhibited between family and friends. However, I couldn't confront the interpreter or the claimant due to my role as an independent medical examiner.

The objectivity of translated content decreases when family members or friends act as interpreters. This is especially true when the interpreter also makes decisions as a guardian or is financially responsible for the patient. For example, in certain subgroups of Asian, Southeast Asian, Middle Eastern, and African cultures, the husband makes medical or financial decisions for his wife. Oftentimes, in these cases, I allow the husband to be in the treatment room to help translate when his wife is receiving treatment. Occasionally, however, I encounter resistance or open objection from the husband about treating the wife, either due to financial reasons or different beliefs. In other words, the husband, being the decision-maker, may vote against treatment on behalf of the wife because he thinks the treatment is either too expensive or unnecessary. In chapter two, I explained the concept of autorejection of treatment based on differences in cultural belief and value system. This is an example of autorejection not by the patient but by the financially responsible party. The husband, then, is the key to case acceptance, as he has the role of interpreter and is also the decision-making family member for the patient. Even scheduling appointments for this patient, who often is a homemaker, can be dependent on the husband's availability around his work schedule.

When I was actively involved with my father's care, I was in the position of being both an interpreter and a caregiver. I was asking questions on behalf of my father and at the same time translating my father's wishes to the doctors and nurses. I was also giving input as a healthcare professional. I was certainly not in a neutral position. But I tried my best to understand which role I was in when.

As a visual for understanding the level of objectivity and subjectivity when dealing with patients and their interpreters, I developed what I call the Objectivity-Subjectivity Gradient of Interpretation Medium, or the OS Gradient.

OBJECTIVITY - SUBJECTIVITY GRADIENT
O - S Gradient

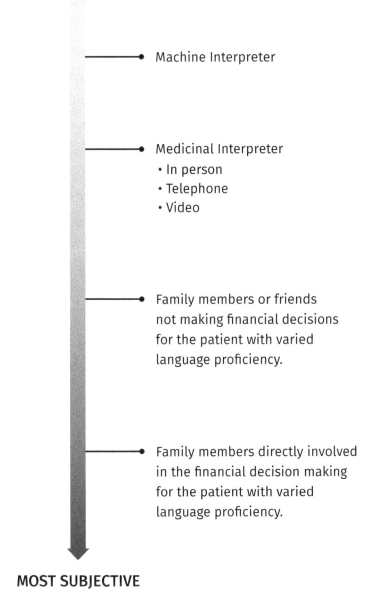

MOST OBJECTIVE

Machine Interpreter

Medicinal Interpreter
• In person
• Telephone
• Video

Family members or friends
not making financial decisions
for the patient with varied
language proficiency.

Family members directly involved
in the financial decision making
for the patient with varied
language proficiency.

MOST SUBJECTIVE

FIGURE 3.1

The OS Gradient (figure 3.1) illustrates the different types of modalities available as an interpretation medium, ranging across a spectrum of objective to subjective. Objectivity decreases as the interpreter's relationship gets closer to the patient; the interpreter interjects opinions, influences a patient's decisions, and becomes especially subjective when they are directly involved in financial responsibilities, transportation arrangements, or caregiving (see diagram).

On the far left of the spectrum is the most objective medium: machine interpreters. As we move toward the right, the medium becomes more subjective. Naturally, machine interpreters—apps or programs that do not involve live persons—will be most objective, as translations are word for word.

Next on the spectrum are professional interpreters. These include certified professional interpreters from an agency. The interpreters are trained to stay objective and often have no personal relationship with the patient. Therefore, it is unlikely that their language will be skewed to sway the patient's decision-making. Medical providers, including doctors, dentists, therapists, nurses, and assistants who work in offices, facilities, or hospitals are professionals equipped with medical knowledge and medical vocabulary who can help facilitate communication effectively. In addition to effective communication, medical professionals and auxiliary staff also actively engage in facilitating the patient's need to expedite paperwork and answer questions aside from those about the treatment itself.

At the right end of the spectrum are family and friends of the patients, who may or may not have financial decision-making power or authority over the patient. When the interpreter is financially responsible for the patient, the decision to go forward with treating the patient lies with the interpreter's ability to pay for the treatment. Therefore, it is most subjective.

MACHINE INTERPRETERS

One might argue that by eliminating the human factor, it is possible to eradicate bias entirely. True, translation apps offer convenience for simple situations, such as the quick search for words, phrases, or simple sentences. But language translation in the healthcare setting has much higher levels of complexity and requires constant interaction, interpretation, and active feedback from all parties, including the patient, the provider, and the interpreter.

For example, I've found that Google Translate is not capable of translating different contexts in some situations. My dentist friend Dr. Nathan Ho developed a great patient-review software program and asked me to check the Chinese-translated version of the review platform. I discovered that Google Translate translated "help" into "mayday" instead of "assistance," and "profile" was translated into "silhouette" instead of "personal data." I am hopeful that future technologies will allow more sophisticated interactive translation apps or programs that can build context into translation in real time, but presently, the human element is still more reliable and fluid.

While hospitals often have phone or video translation services available, these services are still largely lacking in private practice settings. We as providers do the best we can to bridge the gaps. While bias is inevitable, when in need, some interpretation is better than no interpretation. And apps that offer translation can still be beneficial by preserving objectivity.

COMPETENCY AIDS IN QUALITY OF TRANSLATION

The quality of the translation depends on the translator's depth and breadth of knowledge about the healthcare system, common medical and dental procedures and terminology, and their own past experiences and understanding of the subject in question.

Quality translation must have three elements: (1) proper usage of the vocabulary, (2) proper application of the context, and (3) objectivity of the translated content.

The example I mentioned about Google Translate, where "help" was translated into "mayday," violated the first and the second elements of quality translation. Although objective, it didn't make any sense.

Earlier in the chapter, the example of the Korean interpreter clearly violated the third element: objectivity. While I was not able to verify his proper usage of vocabulary nor context, I did not feel that his English proficiency was sufficient to supply me with the precise picture I needed to know for the independent medical exam. I then leaned on the police report and the medical record for objectivity.

When I explain and translate at the same time to my Chinese-speaking patients, I pay attention to how things are worded, the same as in English. For example, I use the word "discomfort" instead of "pain," and "local anesthesia" instead of "needles." Trigger words are the same across cultures and languages, and fear of pain is universal, after all.

CUES OF QUALITY TRANSLATION RUN LIKE MUSICAL PHRASES

Music is universal. Regardless of the instrument, be it piano, bass, saxophone, or vocal, there are musical phrases throughout a passage. Musical phrases allow expressions and moderation in tone, volume, and speed. Rests taken between musical phrases are meant for the musicians to take breaths. I am a trained pianist. My children play low brass instruments. I have very little knowledge about how low brass instruments play. However, I can hear the wrong notes or if breaths are taken in the wrong place because I have a pair of trained ears as a musician. I call out their mistakes to keep them on their toes a bit.

Imagine languages are like different musical instruments. We may not know how to play another instrument, but the basic elements of music or language are there: tone of voice, expressions, phrases marked by pauses.

Now, I am asking you to listen to a foreign language as though you are listening to a song you've never heard before. I am inviting you to listen to the nonverbal elements of speech: intonation, speed, volume, pauses, and affect. When determining the quality of the translation, as a provider, I look for active feedback from the interpreter and the patient as I communicate. I look for cues where I feel that at least the main concepts of my explanation have come across. If the main ideas are understood and accepted successfully, I am then able to fine-tune details.

Let me explain further. If I spend one minute explaining the very basic anatomy of the tooth to the interpreter, I want to know that the key concepts of the layers of the tooth have been explained and understood first by the interpreter, then by the patient. I explain the tooth anatomy starting with the outermost layer, the enamel, then the dentin and the pulp, respectively. I tell the interpreter that enamel, the outermost layer, is the hardest part of the tooth. Dentin is softer and the second layer, and pulp is the center of the tooth, where the tissues and nerve endings live. In translating, I would expect to hear the interpreter explaining these details to the patient in more or less the same or longer amount of time as I did with the interpreter. If I spend one minute explaining a concept in English, it is unlikely that, in any language, the interpreter would be able to translate my concepts in ten seconds, regardless of how compact this language is. Even without me necessarily knowing the other language, I should be able to hear some pauses between each concept about enamel, dentin, and pulp, because explanation of concepts requires step-by-step, layered understanding.

Thus, in the absence of understanding another language, the provider can look for cues such as pauses between sentences and the length of the translation. Ask for feedback to make sure that all the information translated was clear. A picture is worth a thousand words, so I sometimes also draw a simple illustration explaining disease processes to both the interpreter and the patient. The interpreter can point to the picture I draw as he or she explains the layers of a tooth, for example. That helps me to know what has been explained by the interpreter to the patient and can help me see whether certain parts need more clarification. Illustrations also help communication become more successful not just from a language point of view but also by building patient rapport and trust by encouraging active participation from the patient.

Learning language has never been easier. There are various types of resources on the market. Multilingual patient forms and brochures are usually formulated by medical and legal specialists, adding another layer of quality assurance. Various types of handheld portable language translators are also available in stores and online, as are handbooks or textbooks for professionals with Spanish medical terminology. My children's school uses Rosetta Stone programs for its second-language curriculum. Providers are encouraged to learn a second language, or a third. Team members with diverse backgrounds and different language abilities certainly help your days to run more smoothly.

Communication with patients speaking a language other than

English does not stop at translation of the content. Are we translating everything that should be translated? Are we allowed to translate everything to all parties due to patient confidentiality? Is less more? As a healthcare professional, there is another component layered over all communication—the Health Insurance Portability and Accountability Act of 1996, known as HIPAA, which is the US law governing the privacy of patient medical information.

IMPROVE YOUR
Cultural Competency

1. Bias from interpreters exists. The closer the interpreter's relationship to the patient, the more subjective the bias, especially if the interpreter has decision-making power for the patient.

2. The Objectivity-Subjectivity Gradient of Interpretation lists different modalities of interpreters.

3. Current machine-generated interpreters lack the complexity needed to adequately translate medical and dental terminology and information. Context can be skewed.

4. Competency of interpreters varies. Try to find cues to gauge whether main discussion points come across successfully by paying attention to the length of the translation, pauses between concepts, and active feedback and engagement from the patient.

5. Languages are like music. Listening to the nonverbal elements of a foreign language can give you some cues to the quality of the translation without knowing the words.

CHAPTER 4

The HIPAA Dilemma

Confidentiality is the essence of being trusted.

~ **Billy Graham**

I n my office, before performing any surgical procedure, an informed consent form is provided for the patient to sign. An informed consent states the potential risks and complications associated with the procedure. These consents are often drafted by attorneys and specialists with legal knowledge.

In one of my consents, there is a section regarding the potential interaction between birth control and antibiotics. Theoretically, there is a small probability that birth control can be made ineffective by taking the antibiotics given, although it is rare. Therefore, it is best to utilize additional birth control methods while taking antibiotics.

When I provided the informed consent to an eighteen-year-old Chinese woman to sign in front of her parents, she didn't flinch and quickly initialed and signed the consent. However, as soon as her parents stepped out, she whispered to me, "I just want you to know that my parents don't know that I am on birth control, can you please not tell them?" I promised her I wouldn't tell her parents. We discussed the possibility of drug interactions, I documented this in her chart as such, and we proceeded with the procedure, without informing her parents.

As an example, consider the 2019 movie *The Farewell*, which follows first-generation Chinese American Billie, who moved to the US at age six but who goes back to China to visit her grandmother, Nai-Nai, after learning that her grandmother was diagnosed with terminal lung cancer. The family had decided that it was best for Nai-Nai to not know about her own diagnosis. Billie struggled to understand how that was acceptable, raising the point that it's illegal to withhold such information in the US. Billie's father, who has been Americanized, also doubted the group decision, but nevertheless went along with the rest of the family because he understood the tradition. Even the doctor, who was educated in the UK, agreed with the family, saying, "It's a good lie. Most families in China would not tell her." Billie's uncle, Haiban, explained, "In the East, a person's life is part of a whole," and not just experienced on an individual level. Decisions are made collectively as a family, as opposed to the Westernized philosophy of making decisions independently.

The Farewell is an excellent example of how HIPAA can create challenges in certain cultural contexts, as the policy is designed in the American context. If Billie's family had made the same decision here in the US, it would be considered a HIPAA violation. Requests made by family not to disclose medical diagnosis to the patient would have been turned down by medical professionals.

In discussing cross-cultural competency and language interpretation, HIPAA regulations can often make communication between patients and providers lengthier and more complicated.

HIPAA, or the Health Insurance Portability and Accountability Act of 1996, was signed to address several issues in the healthcare industry, including privacy, the security of health information, and the rights of patients to their health information. HIPAA has seven titles. Title II, which is designed to prevent healthcare fraud and abuse, simplify administration, and reform medical liability, mainly affects healthcare providers and our daily practice. The Department of Health and Human Services (DHHS) developed rulings for HIPAA and published a final Privacy Rule in December 2000.

In discussing cross-cultural competency and language interpretation, HIPAA regulations can often make communication between patients and providers lengthier and more complicated.

As of April 2003, compliance with HIPAA has been required for what is defined as "covered entities": healthcare providers, health plans, and healthcare clearinghouses. For the purposes of this chapter, the discussion will focus mainly on the implication of day-to-day cultural and language challenges when it comes to HIPAA.

For healthcare providers, it is important to abide by the general HIPAA regulations, paying special attention to patients with language and cultural barriers. For many healthcare providers working in a multicultural setting, some of the scenarios discussed in this chapter may not be uncommon.

Please note that this chapter is not intended to serve as legal guidance, but it may help to clear up some confusion for providers, especially when it comes to communicating with patients from other cultures. For more information, I encourage you to visit HHS.gov/hipaa.

Before we get into the discussion, it is important to understand the following definitions:

Privacy Rule: The Privacy Rule was issued by DHHS as a set of national standards for the protection of certain health information. The rule requires providers to implement appropriate safeguards to protect patients' personal health information, and it specifies limits and conditions on the way that information may be used and disclosed. It gives patients the right to obtain their health records from a provider and to request corrections to those records. [4]

Protected Health Information (PHI): This is any individually identifiable health information, including a patient's demographics, medical records, and insurance or payment information that is transmitted and maintained by covered entities.

(HIPAA) Covered Entities: As defined by the HIPAA law, this includes healthcare providers, health plans, and healthcare clearinghouses.

Designated Record Set: A group of records maintained by or for a covered entity. This may include medical records, billing records maintained by HIPAA-covered entities, insurance information, clinical lab results, x-rays, clinical notes (subjective, objective, assessment, and plan—SOAP—notes), but NOT psychotherapy notes. Patients do not have access to information outside designated record sets. Examples include patient safety record and quality improvement assessments to improve customer service.

Legal Health Record: There is no regulatory definition for legal

---

"The HIPAA Privacy Rule," US Department of Health and Human Services, accessed October 31, 2019, https://www.hhs.gov/hipaa/for-professionals/privacy/index.html.

health record. These are records for which a provider may receive a subpoena for a certain purpose. These generally include the medical record or the part of a medical record that would be used in court. The provider must determine the intent of the request for the record and produce what's requested in order to avoid penalties.

Emancipated Minor: This is a mechanism by which a child before attaining the age of majority is freed from control by parents or guardians via means of entering a marriage, joining the military, or a court order.

Age of Majority: The age threshold where a minor enters adulthood. In most states, the age of majority is eighteen. However, there are currently a few exceptions: Alabama (nineteen), Nebraska (nineteen), and Mississippi (twenty-one). The age of a minor being able to legally sign for medical consent may also vary depending on the state.

Personal Representatives: Under the Privacy Rule, a personal representative is a person authorized to act on behalf of the individual in making healthcare-related decisions. For example, the parent is the personal representative of a minor child.

Persons with Limited English Proficiency (LEP): These are individuals for whom English is not their primary language and who have difficulty communicating in English.

Notice of Privacy Practices (NOPP): This notice includes how the Privacy Rule allows providers to use and disclose protected health information, the patient's privacy rights, and the organization's duties to protect privacy of health information. Healthcare providers are required to ask the patient for a signature to acknowledge receipt of this notice. Informed consents for clinical care are given separately from NOPP.

Again, please bear in mind that this chapter does not serve as a legal reference and the purpose of these definitions is to help you better understand the rest of the discussion. For more information on the HIPAA laws, go to HHS.gov.

Now let's look at some of the ways HIPAA affects practice today.

THE STANDARD OF "MINIMUM NECESSARY"

Here's a common scenario: you performed a biopsy, blood tests, or radiographic imaging reports. You call the patient to come in, and the call goes to voicemail. What would you leave on that voicemail? Since the implementation of HIPAA, reporting test results may no longer be as simple as making one phone call.

HIPAA's Privacy Rule stresses the standard of "minimum necessary" use and disclosure. What that means is that healthcare providers are required to use the minimum necessary information to achieve their purpose without disclosing the patient's entire medical record for the purpose of the call. This rule applies across the board, with or without a cultural or language barrier.

I've shared some examples of minimum necessary in the section on demystifying HIPAA below.

RULES FOR INTERPRETERS

HIPAA allows providers to share health information with a certified interpreter; an interpreter who works with the provider, such as a bilingual nurse; or an interpreter who is a family member or friend.

The bottom line is that HIPAA allows healthcare providers to discuss health-protected information with *anyone the patient identifies, as long as the patient does not object to the sharing of information.*

DEMYSTIFYING HIPAA

Can language and cultural barriers make HIPAA more complicated? Absolutely. However, by understanding the basic rules involved in HIPAA, communication can also be less cumbersome.

Let's look at some common scenarios providers might deal with in an office or hospital setting to help better understand how HIPAA applies, and what a provider can do to stay in compliance.

MINIMUM NECESSARY

THE SITUATION: Mr. Patel had a biopsy and he expressed his worries about having cancer. You received Mr. Patel's biopsy result and it is premalignant. You need Mr. Patel to come in to discuss further, but the voicemail picked up. What do you do?

THE SOLUTION: When you call Mr. Patel and get a voicemail, the best sort of message is along the lines of, "Mr. Patel, this is Dr. Good's office reaching out to you regarding your biopsy result. Please give us a call back at your convenience." If Mr. Patel picks up the phone at that moment, the healthcare provider may then discuss in more detail with the patient only after confirming that the person answering the call is the patient himself, Mr. Patel.

ANOTHER SITUATION: You received a letter from an attorney requesting a "medical record" because your patient initiated a suit against another provider (if the suit is against you, contact your malpractice insurance right away to discuss further). You are not sure how much information to include. What do you send?

THE SOLUTION: Read the attorney's letter closely, decide on the intent for the request, and produce what's minimally necessary for the purpose of the request when disclosing information permitted by HIPAA. HIPAA does not specify what constitutes "legal medical record." In general, this may be the patient's partial or full medical record or billing record, which may include health information, clinical notes, lab results and x-rays, and financial statements. Failure to respond may subject you to sanction. The provider must determine the purpose of the request and follow the "minimum necessary" rule. Sending too much information may violate HIPAA. Typically, the letter from the attorney gives clear instructions of what needs to be included in the reply.

OTHER PROVIDER'S RECORDS

THE SITUATION: Mr. Patel is moving to Arizona to live with his son. He requested and authorized that you forward his medical record to his new doctor. Mr. Patel has a long-standing medical history and you have copies from his other physicians. May you include those medical records from other physicians?

THE SOLUTION: Yes, the Privacy Rule permits a provider who is a covered entity to disclose a complete medical record, including portions that were created by another provider, assuming that the disclosure is for a purpose permitted by the Privacy Rule, such as treatment.

REFUSAL TO SIGN

THE SITUATION: A thirty-five-year-old Albanian woman comes in for an appointment. Her husband has come along as her translator. He refuses to sign the Notice of Privacy Practices. He is upset and says to you, "I don't understand what this is and I am not signing this." His wife is shaking her head to you as well. May you still proceed with treatment?

THE SOLUTION: Treatment consents are separate from HIPAA consents. When the patient refuses to sign the HIPAA notice, document in the chart that you have given the notice and that the patient refused to sign. HIPAA requires a "good faith effort" to obtain a signature. It does not prevent a provider from using or disclosing the history of present illness (HPI). "Good faith effort" means that you have tried to explain the importance of this document and tried to obtain a signature from the patient.

DISCUSSING TREATMENT OF AN ADULT PATIENT WITH PARENTS

THE SITUATION: A twenty-year-old female Egyptian patient is attending college out of state. Her parents have called and expressed concern that her wisdom tooth was hurting and her face is beginning to swell. You saw the patient two months ago in your office, and her parents came in with her at that time. Her parents are financially responsible for her. You want to converse with the patient to make some suggestions about what she can do in her situation, but she doesn't answer when you call her phone. Can you communicate with her parents, since she's over eighteen?

THE SOLUTION: Yes, you can speak with the parents about the patient, since two months ago you saw her in your office with her parents present. Even without the patient present now, you can discuss her care with her parents. The HIPAA Privacy Rule states that healthcare providers (covered entities) are allowed to share information with family members identified by the patient about the patient's care or payment for healthcare. Providers may use their best judgment to make suggestions as needed. Consider asking the patient if she has no objections to sharing information with her parents, even if the parents are not financially responsible for the patient.

A NEIGHBOR AS REPRESENTATIVE

THE SITUATION: You extracted wisdom teeth for a forty-nine-year-old Indian woman and provided intravenous sedation in the office. The patient speaks Hindi, and her neighbor drove her to the appointment and is also acting as her translator. Are you allowed to go over instructions with her neighbor?

THE SOLUTION: The answer is yes. The HIPAA Privacy Rule allows involvement of friends or other persons identified by a patient. A doctor may give information to a friend if the patient has mobility limitations and needs a ride from a facility to home.

PICKING UP PRESCRIPTIONS ON A PATIENT'S BEHALF

THE SITUATION: The same Indian woman's neighbor calls one hour after leaving the appointment she was at with the patient. She states that they forgot to pick up prescriptions for the patient. Is it okay for that neighbor to return to pick up prescriptions on the patient's behalf?

THE SOLUTION: Since this person came as an escort for the patient, the doctor may allow her to pick up the prescriptions on the patient's behalf. The doctor may also give instructions to the neighbor about the dosing and frequency of the medications, because the neighbor has been identified by the patient.

DISCUSSING DAD WITH ADULT DAUGHTER

THE SITUATION: An eighty-one-year-old Jewish man living in a nursing home came in for his appointment with his daughter and his aide. He is scheduled two weeks out for his procedure. However, his daughter calls the day before the procedure, saying that her father just had a heart attack and now is hospitalized. Are you allowed to discuss further plans with his daughter?

THE SOLUTION: Yes. According to HIPAA's Privacy Rule, a doctor may discuss an incapacitated patient's condition with a family member over the phone.

DISCUSSING BILLING WITH FAMILY

THE SITUATION: The front desk billing specialist checked your eighty-one-year-old incapacitated patient's account while on the phone with his daughter. They forgot to pay the man's copay the last time they were in the office. May the front desk billing specialist discuss this issue with the patient's daughter?

THE SOLUTION: Yes. The HIPAA Privacy Rule allows discussion of payment with a family member, in the office or hospital.

TREATING A MARRIED TEEN: EMANCIPATED MINORS

THE SITUATION: A sixteen-year-old, pregnant, Spanish-speaking female comes in with her husband to be seen for an abscessed tooth. Her husband, who is twenty-three years old, translates for her. May you treat this patient without her parents? Can she sign her own medical consent?

THE SOLUTION: Yes. Minors are emancipated in the following situations: marriage, active military service, or court order. However, states have different regulations and rules. Check with your state regulations to ensure that the individual is emancipated under your state's law.

PATIENT OBJECTS TO SHARING INFORMATION

THE SITUATION: A twenty-five-year-old Chinese American PhD student comes in for consultation about his jaw pain. His parents are with him in the room during the consultation. The parents are very inquisitive and actively involved in the discussion. After the consultation, the patient asks to speak with you privately. He discloses that he was recently diagnosed with schizophrenic affective disorder and he doesn't want his parents to know because it's shameful in Chinese culture to be identified with mental disease. His family pays for his treatment. What should you do?

THE SOLUTION: You are not allowed to discuss any information with others if the patient objects. Ask the patient if there is anything else that he does not want to disclose to the parents. Note in chart what you are allowed or not allowed to discuss. Flag the account so that your staff members are all aware of this.

PATIENT LIVING IN A FACILITY WITH COURT PAPERS

THE SITUATION: Seventeen-year-old Yasmine came in for a wisdom teeth consult. She lives in a youth home. Her staff member was with her. You were told that her parents were divorced. Her mother usually signs her consent, but her father is financially responsible for her treatment. She does not live with her parents. How do you proceed?

THE SOLUTION: Ask the staff member for copies of court papers indicating the legal guardianship and financially responsible party for this patient. Obtain copies of the legal paperwork before treatment is rendered. Clarify with the facility whom you should contact based on the court order.

CONSEQUENCES OF A HIPAA VIOLATION

I still remember clearly that one of the first things I learned during my internship year of residency was to keep quiet in the hospital elevator. No discussing of Mrs. Smith's bloodwork or Mr. Jones's surgery in the open. As healthcare practitioners, we try hard to make conscious efforts to abide by HIPAA rules. Despite our best efforts, violations can occur, and consequences are often grave.

In 2010, Huping Zhou, a former cardiothoracic surgeon in China who was employed at UCLA, was terminated due to work-performance reasons.[5] Following his termination, he accessed numerous medical records of his former coworkers, as well as Hollywood celebrities, without permission. He ultimately pleaded guilty to four counts of misdemeanor of HIPAA violation. While Zhou's violations

---

5   "Ex-UCLA Healthcare Employee Pleads Guilty to Four Counts of Illegally Peeking at Patient Records," Federal Bureau of Investigation, accessed January 11, 2020, https://archives.fbi.gov/archives/losangeles/press-releases/2010/la010810a.htm.

appeared to be intentional, there are other circumstances where violations could be acts of carelessness. For example, several hospitals were fined simply for filming patients without obtaining consents.

In our daily practice, HIPAA can be violated by any member of the team. It is therefore important to educate your team members. Whenever possible, the rule of minimum necessary should apply when it comes to patient communication. This can simply happen when your receptionist repeats someone's social security number out loud over the phone in an open area where other patients can hear that information. A HIPAA officer should be appointed in each practice.

Some of the most common reasons for HIPAA violations include:

- Openly discussing health-protected information or gossiping about a patient

- Unauthorized release or access of health-protected information

- Improper storage of health-protected information (paper or electronic)

- Loss of data due to breach

In other words, some examples of violations include: employees discussing a patient's medical condition out loud in the open, computer hacking, exposing charts in an openly accessible area, or emailing the wrong person about someone else's information.

It is not uncommon to have names with similar spellings or even the same spellings. My first name is Cathy, but it can be misspelled as "Cathie," "Kathy," or "Kathie." Ethnic names may be even more confusing to many. It's common for father and son to share the same name. Most health organizations will utilize photo ID and date of birth to identify the individual. It is also possible that patients with similar names may present a similar physical status and have similar procedures done around the same period of time. Imagine calling the wrong Mr. Patel to inform him over the phone that he might have cancer.

Train your staff members to be mindful when checking in patients. Double check the spelling of the name, especially when spelling differences are minor, such as "Gonzalez" versus "Gonzales," "Cheng" versus "Chang," and "Ahmed" versus "Ahmad."

There are many complicated scenarios and other discussions about HIPAA that are beyond the scope of this chapter. However, I hope I have helped to clarify some of them for you. Again, to learn more about HIPAA and how it might affect your practice, visit HHS.gov.

IMPROVE YOUR
Cultural Competency

Here are some of the general rules of good practice when it comes to HIPAA:

1. When a patient refuses to sign any form of documentation, document in the chart that you have tried and the patient refused. We must make a "good faith effort" to obtain a signature.

2. Refusal to sign a HIPAA notice does not preclude providers from rendering treatment.

3. As long as the patient *does not object* to the discussion, the general rules for communicating with interpreters as family and friends are that the provider may discuss with the person the patient identifies prescription pickup, ride

home, instructions for medications, etcetera. It is good practice to note the name of the person who accompanies the patient.

4. Health information for adult children may be discussed with parents who are caring and financially responsible for the patient, as long as the patient does not object.

5. The provider may discuss payment or financial information with family members, especially in situations where adult children are taking care of elderly patients and may be financially responsible for the payment.

6. Providers are to use their best professional judgment when communicating with patients for use and disclosure of protected health information under the HIPAA Privacy Rule.

7. Certain cases may be accompanied by court papers. These include divorce or minors living in facilities due to behavioral, mental health, or drug rehab reasons. For these cases, check with custodial parents, case managers, and facilities and proceed according to instructions.

8. Emancipated minors due to marriage, joining the military, or court orders may sign medical consents on their own. Check your state law for further details. In most states, the age of majority is eighteen, with a few exceptions.

9. Spellings of names can be confusing, especially ethnic names. Same names are not uncommon. Use photo ID and date of birth to further identify individuals with each encounter to avoid mistakes.

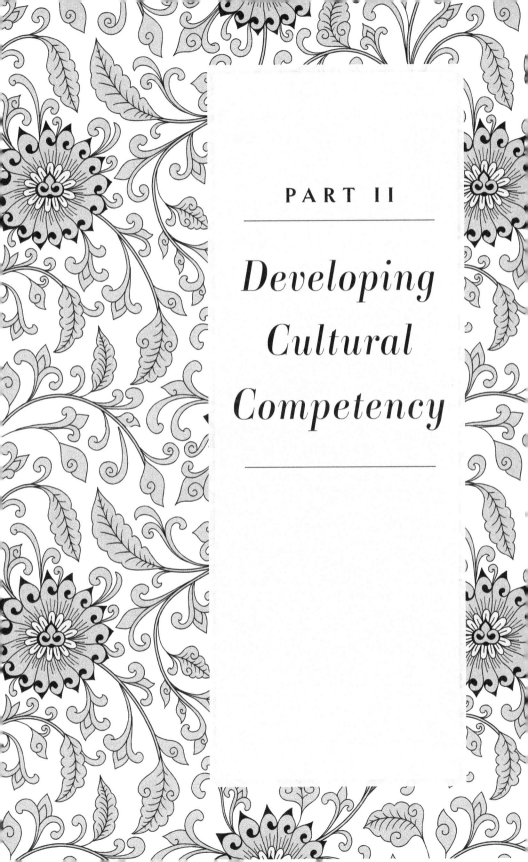

PART II

Developing Cultural Competency

CHAPTER 5

Breaking Through the Cultural Niche

If you talk to a man in a language he understands,
that goes to his head. If you talk to him in
his language, that goes to his heart.

~ **Nelson Mandela**

So far, we have learned to be better observers and better communicators by raising our awareness of different styles of cultural communication. We have learned about the theory of second-language acquisition, for which everyone has their own unique Chain of Zigzags. We have learned about the Dichotomy of Treatment Trust that can occur due to cultural differences. We also need to follow general rules of HIPAA, in addition to navigating the challenges from cultural and language barriers. Are we, the healthcare providers, doing everything possible to bridge the gaps? Is it truly possible to break cultural niches?

My practice is referral based, which by definition is B2B (business to business). I do have a number of patients who find me from searching the internet or who are recommended by family and friends through word of mouth, but most of my referrals come from general dentists' offices. Being in the business for more than fifteen years, I have observed that frequently doctors of the same or similar racial backgrounds refer to one another. This is understandable, due to having similar language, cultural, or religious beliefs, especially for first-generation doctors and patients. Communication is made easier by referring to someone who has fewer language, cultural, or religious barriers, which also helps to increase patient satisfaction.

My own first-generation, Chinese-speaking patients often say to me, "We are so glad we've found you. We couldn't find another Chinese-speaking specialist like you in this area who also took our insurance. It's so much easier to communicate this way."

TOWNS BY THE CULTURE

With all that I've shared with you, it may surprise you to know that Chinese-speaking patients do not make up the majority of my practice. I have a large percentage of first-generation immigrants in my practice who speak different languages, including regional dialects: Gujarati, Punjabi, Urdu, Hindu, Arabic, Russian, Polish, Spanish, Mandarin Chinese, Cantonese, and Korean, among others. In the central New Jersey area, where my practice is located, there are several large cultural groups in the community: Indians speaking different languages, Chinese (mostly from mainland China), Jewish (largely Russian), and Egyptian (both Muslim and Christian), to name a few. In northern New Jersey, there are large cultural communities you can identify by the names of towns. For example, Newark and Elizabeth have large numbers of Spanish and Portuguese immigrants, whereas Paramus and Fort Lee are well-known for their large Korean communities.

Generally, when the name of the town is associated with a specific culture, it defines the demographics of the town. Therefore, one should not be surprised to find more Korean doctors, especially first-generation Korean doctors, in practice in the town of Fort Lee, servicing first-generation immigrants from South Korea. The term "Korean Town" is no longer necessary and becomes redundant because it's a well-known fact. Therefore, it is only natural for Korean doctors to refer patients to one another within the vicinity. Why refer to someone outside the cultural group, where language and cultural barriers are harder to break?

Yet, when you walk around areas like these with a specific and strong cultural presence, you can find a high level of diversity and inclusion, especially where food is involved. Around New Brunswick, New Jersey, where Rutgers University campuses are, you can walk down a street and see a wide variety of restaurants comfortably situated adjacent to one another: Mexican, Greek, Italian, Chinese, Mediterranean, and Indian along with Irish pubs and American steakhouses. The socioeconomic implication spells supply–demand; every community needs a variety of multicultural businesses that represent the people who reside in the area. The patrons of different restaurants are of different racial backgrounds.

Looking at these cultural landscapes raises a couple of questions: First, if I were to decide to move to a town in homogeneous America that has one Chinese takeout place and where people turn their heads to look at me because I am the only Asian person in the supermarket, would I have a shot at establishing a successful practice compared to practitioners with the same beliefs as their patients? And second, if I were to decide to move to a town with different immigrants for whom English is a second language and the people in town have very different cultural beliefs and practices from my own, would I feel comfortable relating to people on a daily basis?

SHARING COMMONALITIES CAN HELP US SEE THROUGH ONE ANOTHER'S EYES

An Indian friend of mine from Mumbai once told me, "I'll tell you a secret: we Indians, as patients, will come to you because we still relate to each other as Asians."

This statement came up during a casual conversation, and his personal opinions were surprising, reassuring, and comforting to me as a friend, but also brought up interesting points. My friend continued to elaborate that we (the Indians and the Chinese) both believe in respecting the elderly and respecting professionals, such as doctors and engineers. Both cultures have long histories and have numerous subcultures and dialects.

In other words, sharing cultural values helps to break the barrier and helps individuals identify with one another. Keeping an open mind to learning about another culture is the key. My Indian friend felt comfortable bonding with me because of our shared cultural beliefs.

When it comes to treating patients, recognizing cultural groups who share common beliefs can definitely be a great starting point, even before your patients learn about you as an individual. Exposing yourself to different cultures by making friends with people from different backgrounds, reading books about different cultures, and traveling are all great ways to expand your understanding.

Avoid falling into traps of stereotypes. My first-generation, Italian, immigrant husband often expresses to me that he's displeased at being stereotyped as "mafioso" from *The Sopranos* TV series. As an interracial couple, we often get questions like, "So what do you eat at home?" as if Chinese people should only eat or cook Chinese food and Italians should only eat or cook Italian food. In fact, there are many commonalities between the two cuisines. One could easily draw parallels between pasta and noodles or ravioli and dumplings, for example. And in our household, we may have chicken marsala on Monday, fried rice on Tuesday, osso buco on Wednesday (served over gnocchi or rice), dumplings on Thursday, and pizza from around the corner on Friday. Our children are exposed to Italian and Chinese cultures equally, and their best friends in school are Indians.

FOOD BRINGS PEOPLE TOGETHER

One reason I continue to mention food is that it creates conversation, brings warmth and joy, and is the easiest topic to bond people together, even if a language barrier exists.

One of the earliest examples of immigrants using food to bond with others and break stereotypes was Mr. Johnny Kan, owner of Johnny Kan's restaurant in San Francisco's Chinatown in 1953. Johnny Kan introduced authentic Chinese cooking and the use of the lazy Susan to the region. His restaurant was frequented by celebrities such as Danny Kaye, Craig Claiborne, and even Frank Sinatra and Marilyn Monroe. Kan was the among the first to break the stereotype of Americanized imitations of Chinese items like chop suey.

My Russian cosmetician friend, Snezhenna, told me about a nearby supermarket, NetCost Market, which offers hot and cold bars of premade delicacies from Russia and other Eastern European areas—foods such as borscht soup, liver salad, salmon shuba salad, and Napoleon cake. I've had many Russian patients and, no matter how anxious and stressed they are, when we talk about the food at NetCost, it brings a smile to their faces. We talk about the ethnic food offered there before their teeth are extracted and about what food they may be able to eat afterward.

The other reason I talk about food is because it can help you to easily identify the demographics of the area by simply driving around town. Bilingual signs and ethnic food restaurants can be an indication of the demographics of a community. If you are newly settled in town, take some time to learn about your patients' cultural groups so that you can enhance your communication skills to relate to them.

Again, food is a great common denominator in day-to-day human interactions. Elizabeth Gilbert, author of the book *Eat, Pray, Love*, knew that, and as a result, her work was wildly successful (maybe you've seen the movie with Julia Roberts?). In her book, she narrated her traveling experience with her exquisite and captivating writing abilities, highlighting human sensorial experience through visuals, sounds, smells, and tastes.

BREAKING THE CULTURAL NICHE: IS IT POSSIBLE?

Cultural competency enhances communication and bridges the gaps by reducing resistance and mistrust, therefore increasing treatment outcome success.

Can the cultural niche be broken? Would a patient from a different background still come to you even though you are different than they are?

The answer is yes. You are a healthcare provider with clinical skills and knowledge to treat your patients and solve the problems they have. Cultural competency enhances communication and bridges the gaps by reducing resistance and mistrust, therefore increasing treatment outcome success. When a patient feels comfortable and starts to develop trust because you are not being biased or judgmental about their culture, that patient will most likely return to you for following visits, and possibly refer their friends and family.

Certainly, cultural niches are harder to break when you are entering a tight-knit community where providers and patients are of the same cultural origin and perhaps religious practices. When I worked in a Jewish practice, many patients would come to see the owner of the practice because they went to the same congregation. When they saw me, a younger Asian woman, walk into the treatment room, the automatic rejection—the Dichotomy of Treatment Trust mentioned in chapter two—often kicked in. A few patients would flat out refuse to see me and even wanted to be rescheduled. One female patient, in particular, yelled at me and told me to get out of the room. In some instances, you may certainly find a deeply rooted belief that a doctor from the inner circle is far superior to an outsider. In those instances, I found that patients didn't care whether I went through the same educational process to achieve equivalent credentials. In their mind, they had already identified the best practitioner for them, and their choice was tied in with their cultural and religious beliefs.

Most of the time, though, despite the initial disappointment of not being able to see the owner of the practice, the majority of patients would give me the benefit of the doubt, carry on with the discussion, and then let me treat them. Most would also decide to return to me for further treatment because we had established initial trust. Some would even apologize and say, "I didn't mean to be rude, it's just that I didn't expect to see you."

Many group practices hire doctors, nurses, and other staff

members from different cultural backgrounds so that the practice can provide care to patients of different backgrounds. If you are a solo practitioner like myself, it is especially important that you do not limit yourself to staying in the comfort zone, but broaden your horizon and learn about other cultural groups. Hiring a diverse team is one way to do this. Later in the book, I'll talk more about ways to help your staff broaden the horizon of your practice, because America is becoming more diverse by the minute.

David Livermore's book, *Leading with Cultural Intelligence*, talks about ten different "cultural clusters" around the world. He proposes that each of the clusters "has similar patterns of thinking and behavior."[6] He also cautions against stereotyping. For example, what he calls "Confucius Asia" includes China, Hong Kong, Japan, Singapore, South Korea, and Taiwan. He proposes that these countries share the Confucian way of thinking and behaving. Drawing from my personal experience, this is certainly valid. Common values, social etiquette, behaviors, and thinking patterns are shared when I treat patients from these areas.

YOU ARE ALL THE SAME; THEREFORE, YOU ALL SHOULD KNOW ONE ANOTHER

I have a fair number of senior patients who are veterans. In many cases, the first time they met me, they asked, "Are you from China/Philippines/Japan/Vietnam?" The assumption of a certain Asian country was usually due to their own internal reference based on where they were stationed. Rarely is someone familiar with my hometown of Taipei, Taiwan. The old name "Formosa" or "Ilha

---

6   David Livermore, *Leading with Cultural Intelligence: The Real Secret to Success* (New York: American Management Association, 2015), 234.

Formosa," meaning "beautiful island," was given by the Portuguese in the 16th century. Some people are familiar with the old country Formosa from more than a half century ago, but not necessarily the metropolitan city I grew up in. Occasionally, after I state where I came from, the patient might then say, "My neighbor is from Hong Kong, do you know her?" or "When I was in Vietnam, I met ___. You remind me of her."

As our nation is becoming more diverse, I find it very important to avoid "you all look the same" conversations. Instead, I encourage open-ended questions when getting to know each other:

- Where are you from?

- How long have you been here in this country?

- Tell me about your town, is it busy or quiet?

- What language do you speak?

- How did you learn English?

- How long have you been in this country?

- How do you pronounce your name? Am I saying it right?

- Can you recommend to me a good restaurant to try? Where does your family go to buy food from back home?

These are some general rules to use when communicating across cultures:

Use active listening. Listen to your patients when they talk. You don't know what you don't know.

Avoid "look-alike" comments. Try not to draw reference from a similar culture to understand the patient's country of origin as though they are the same. It is better to ask questions directly pertaining to this patient's culture and country of origin. For example, if this patient states he is from Pakistan and you comment how much he looks like your Indian friend, the conversation becomes awkward.

Avoid certain topics of conversation and understand basic religious practice rules. In general, avoid discussion of religion or politics for the purpose of conversation. If the religious practices of the patient affect your treatment planning or scheduling, make a note of it. For example, practicing Jewish patients will not pick up their phone between Friday sundown and Saturday sundown; therefore, they will not be your Saturday patients. If the patient is a Jehovah's Witness, they may refuse blood products, so it's important to have an alternative plan to transfusion.

Don't stereotype. Avoid comments that reflect stereotypes. In chapter one, I talked about comments such as "you are so quiet" or "you are tiny because you are Asian." Remember: quietness may be related to English proficiency rather than a personality trait. These comments are not relevant to your treatment and can sound derogatory.

Referring back to my Indian friend who felt that we shared common beliefs, even if he does not belong to my "cultural cluster," the shared values of respect for the elderly and for professionals were strong enough for us to relate across cultures.

BREAK THE NICHE, BUILD REFERRALS

As I mentioned, once you have established relationships with your patients, friend and family referrals will most likely follow. In the recent past, a man brought his Arabic-only-speaking mother to me for treatment. According to him, she had very bad experiences in Egypt. Her son told me that, in their hometown, people died from dental treatment. She was frantic and shaking like a leaf at the thought of being treated. We spent more time than usual between the translation and stop-and-go, making sure she was comfortable. Her son stayed in the treatment room to translate and reassure her. As far as I could tell, he was also a great interpreter. Her son was very courteous and thankful throughout the whole process. During the following visit, this patient found that her recovery from the procedure was uneventful. Her son told me she had no pain and the bleeding was minimal. She came in three weeks after the treatment for a follow-up visit with a smile on her face. Through her son's translation, she told me that everything went fine and that she would come to me—only me—for more treatment because I was kind to her.

By the same token, when I need to refer patients out for specialty services, patients often ask me whether I know anyone speaking their language. Most provider and insurance websites list languages that the doctor or the provider's offices speak. This information can certainly provide value if the patient feels strongly about wanting someone speaking their language. Oftentimes, if the patient is being referred to a hospital, video or phone interpreter services are also available.

However, if I don't personally know a specialist in their culture, but I feel that the specialist doctor I want them to see is the best in my opinion, I will reassure patients on my end. This specialist doctor may be of a different culture, religion, or race, but they have expertise in the area the patient needs specialization in. My referral is then based on my trust for the specialist's training and knowledge rather than language or cultural background.

Breaking into a cultural niche is not impossible, but it requires work. It requires a keen sense of awareness and active effort from the provider. I sometimes take a few minutes to try to break the barrier by asking patients about their customs and holidays, such as Diwali, the Hindu festival of lights, because it's fascinating and I want to know more. Diwali is not relevant to any of the procedures I perform. However, while the patient is telling me a story about how the light protects from darkness and knowledge triumphs over ignorance, something beautiful comes to mind for them and, for a moment, they forget about all the anxiety and concerns associated with the procedure.

The minute a person sets foot on a foreign land that is to become a place they call home, the processes of cultural assimilation and cultural amalgamation start to unfold. *Fresh Off the Boat*, a popular all-Asian TV sitcom aired by ABC during 2015–2019, narrates the story of Eddie Huang, a Taiwanese American lawyer and restaurant entre-preneur who was born in Washington, DC, and moved to Orlando, Florida. The TV comedy series often showed cultural conflicts across generations between the two Taiwanese immigrant parents and the American-born children raised in a "white" neighborhood.

In the next two chapters, we will learn about how cultural assim-ilation and the amalgamation process affect individuals who arrive in this country at different periods of their lives, and how socialization at different periods may affect their intrinsic value systems.

IMPROVE YOUR
Cultural Competency

1. There's a cultural niche when it comes to referrals. Doctors are more likely to refer to other doctors of a similar cultural background and language.

2. It's not impossible to break the cultural niche. It takes effort from the provider to learn about the demographics of the area where the practice is located.

3. Avoid "you are all the same" conversations. Ask open-ended questions to encourage a two-way conversation.

4. Referrals need not follow a pattern based on cultures or countries of origins. Patients should be educated that they are being referred to practitioners with qualified credentials.

CHAPTER 6

The Amalgamation Scale

Assimilation is really a psychological process where you
come to identify with a new country as yours. The ease of
overseas travel and information access interferes with that.

**~ Mark Krikorian, Executive Director of
Center for Immigration Studies**

According to *Merriam-Webster*, the differences between
acculturation, assimilation, and amalgamation are as
follows:

ACCULTURATION is one of several forms of
culture contact, and has a couple of closely related terms,
including assimilation and amalgamation. Although
all three of these words refer to changes due to contact
between different cultures, there are notable differences
between them. Acculturation is often tied to political
conquest or expansion and is applied to the process of
change in beliefs or traditional practices that occurs when
the cultural system of one group displaces that of another.

ASSIMILATION refers to the process through which individuals and groups of differing heritages acquire the basic habits, attitudes, and mode of life of an embracing culture.

AMALGAMATION refers to a blending of cultures, rather than one group eliminating another (acculturation) or one group mixing itself into another (assimilation).[7]

An extreme example of acculturation is Qin Shi Huang, or the First Emperor of Qin. The notorious tyrant Qin Shi Huang is well-known in history for building the initial Great Wall of China, which has been destroyed and rebuilt several times in history. The First Imperial Dynasty of Qin marked the first unification of China. During a short period of ruling (220–206 BC), Qin Shi Huang was able to unify several major systems through domination and violence. He proposed legalism over Confucianism. He abolished education because he believed that too much education led to opposition of his authority and possibly rebellion. Scholars were killed and thousands of books were burned. He also unified the measuring, writing, and currency systems for the first time in Chinese history. In history books, the phrase "same length cart axles, same writing script" described the following: all cart axles must have the same measurements because carriers with different length axles made different tracks on dirt roads, making traveling difficult. All writing was standardized to the Small Seal Script, which has become one of the main scripts used today in calligraphy. Currency was unified; what is known today as the prototype of a Chinese coin—round on the outside with a square inside—was created by Emperor Qin. Among his other major contributions were weaponry and irrigation systems. He accomplished these within a mere fifteen years of beginning his rule; as you can

---

7   "Acculturation," *Merriam-Webster*, accessed December 2, 2019, https://www.merriam-webster.com/dictionary/acculturation.

imagine, he governed these projects of massive scale with extreme force and brutality.

In the modern world, acculturation by force is not condoned. Instead, we often see a mixture of assimilation and amalgamation because most immigrants carry and maintain their cultural heritage while learning about the new culture—American. The degree of assimilation and amalgamation, in my own personal experience, varies depending on the parts of the country where immigrants may disperse differently.

For example, coastal cities such as San Francisco, Los Angeles, New York City, and Miami attract immigrants due to ease of travel and their cosmopolitan atmosphere. There are greater immigrant populations residing in the surrounding suburban towns as well. For example, the Bay Area, between San Francisco and San Jose, has a large Asian immigrant population because of the affinity for high-tech job opportunities in Silicon Valley and the attraction of highly prestigious colleges such as Stanford and the University of California in San Francisco and Berkeley. First-generation immigrants arrive to find jobs for themselves and plan for their children to attend quality schools. While there is a gradual blending of the native heritage with newly learned American culture, many immigrant groups—Chinese (Taiwan, Hong Kong, and mainland China), Indian, Japanese, and Mexican, to name a few—also coexist relatively peacefully.

However, sometimes things don't turn out well. I first came to this country in 1992, during the period of the Los Angeles riots and the destruction of Koreatown. A law-enforcement issue involving different racial groups quickly turned wrong. Violence ensued between African Americans and Korean Americans. Many immigrants seeking a better life—coming to the United States for their American Dream—were shocked and disbelieving to have their dreams shattered. Misunderstandings and resentment between the two racial groups due to their differences and lack of understanding were built into day-to-day interactions and somehow triggered and ignited by the wrong match. Rebuilding infrastructure did not erase the hurt and mistrust that had happened, and it took many more years to rebuild harmony within the community.

Having moved from the West Coast to the East Coast and traveled often within the continental US over the years, I've observed that there is often more cultural assimilation (mixing into a larger group) in towns or cities where there is a smaller immigrant population, and more amalgamation (blending of cultures) where there is a larger immigrant population in the area. Again, this is evident in examples such as the invention of fusion cuisine. We have come very far from the era of moo shu pork and fortune cookies. In 2011, Peter Yen from San Francisco introduced the concept of a Sushirrito, a roll-up with sashimi, rice, and other fresh ingredients, such as guacamole, tempura flakes, and pickled cucumber, in the form of a burrito. His idea was to speed up the slow process of making sushi rolls by putting everything into burrito form in order to serve the busy lunch crowd. The state of Hawai'i, one of the most diverse states in the US, is well-known for originating the poke bowl, a Hawaiian dish with Japanese influence made of diced-up sashimi-grade fish over rice, dressed and mixed with other fresh vegetables, as well as musubi, which is fried Spam over rice wrapped with seaweed in the form of sushi (or nigiri, to be accurate). The popularity of fusion cuisine also piques the curiosity of mainstream America to take a sneak peek into another culture to see what's there. Food, again, serves as the lowest common denominator in breaking boundaries.

Assimilation and amalgamation are not mutually exclusive; they occur concurrently. In the more homogeneous part of America, there is a more natural tendency, or rather expectation, for immigrants who are true minorities by number to adapt to mainstream America. Financial writer Adam McCann compared six major diversity categories across all states in the US: socioeconomic, cultural, religious, political, economic, and household diversity.[8] The results were not surprising: coastal states ranked higher or

Assimilation and amalgamation are not mutually exclusive; they occur concurrently.

highest in diversity, and the middle of the country ranked lower or lowest. From a healthcare provider's point of view, understanding which part of the country you are in and how diverse your state or local community is raises awareness of the challenges you may face in bridging the gaps with your patients. This can be in a situation where you practice in a homogenous community in which treating immigrant patients of heritages other than yours is not a common occurrence, or you may practice in a very diverse community with patients of different backgrounds but have an upbringing that did not expose you to other cultures. The US Census Bureau American Community Survey in 2016 showed that, other than English and Spanish, Chinese was the most common language spoken at home with nearly 3.4 million speakers, followed by Tagalog with 1.7 million. The 2017 American Community Survey (figure 6.1) showed that, by state, the most commonly spoken non-English and non-Spanish languages were German in nine states and French and Vietnamese in six states; in the state of New Jersey, it was Gujarati.

---

8   "Most and Least Diverse States in America," Adam McCann, September 17, 2019, https://wallethub.com/edu/most-least-diverse-states-in-america/38262/.

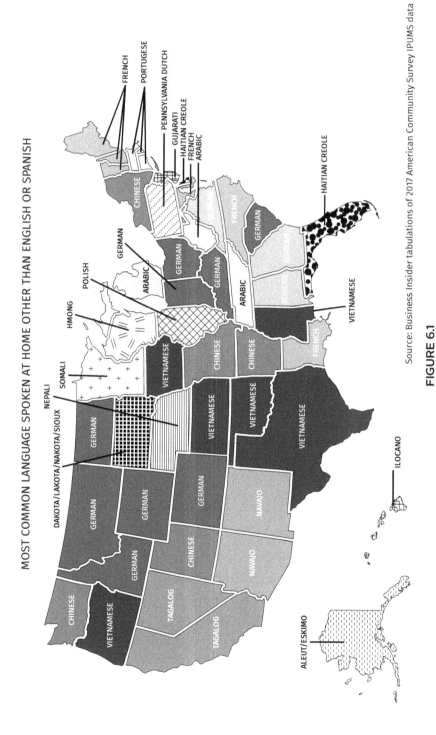

MOST COMMON LANGUAGE SPOKEN AT HOME OTHER THAN ENGLISH OR SPANISH

Source: Business Insider tabulations of 2017 American Community Survey IPUMS data

FIGURE 6.1

Data such as this will help you understand your local demographics and your patients' cultural characteristics.

A NEW CONCEPT

The US Census Bureau predicts that, by 2044, there will no longer be a single ethnic majority. This finding is significant, since 2044 is not that far away from today. Understanding the gradual cultural adaptation process of immigrants will help us to bridge the gaps between healthcare providers and patients. As I shared in chapter one, the acquisition of a second language is not a straight line or curve, but rather a Chain of Zigzags. Each person has a different chain depending on when the second language is acquired and at which stage of socialization the process occurs.

Based on my own experience, I have developed what I call the Amalgamation Scale. The scale is a classification based on the age at and time period during which the individual migrates to the country and the degree of cultural adaptation based on the chronicity of being in the US. The Amalgamation Scale predicts how strongly an individual is rooted in his or her home country and cultural values. The more rooted a person is, the more difficult it may be for them to understand American values and to learn the English language. This scale can help perceive the difficulty they will have with both language and cultural communication.

The Amalgamation Scale can be utilized in any social interaction or work environment, including job interviews, to predict the ease (or difficulty) of communication and possible outcome in terms of language and culture. In explaining the scale, I will focus on the communication between healthcare providers and patients.

Why is this important? In the context of patient relations,

understanding how rooted a person is in his or her culture can help a healthcare provider to gauge (1) how much of a language barrier one might have in understanding the conversation, (2) how likely a patient is to perceive the American system as different from his or her native health system, and (3) how resistant or accepting this person might be to the treatment options proposed, especially when the cultural beliefs of a certain treatment modality may be very different from the American ones.

For the Amalgamation Scale, I use the term "first generation" as defined by the US Census Bureau:

> First generation, or foreign born: anyone who is not a US citizen at birth. This includes naturalized citizens, legal permanent residents, temporary migrants (such as foreign-born students), humanitarian migrants (such as refugees), and undocumented migrants.[9]

The Amalgamation Scale has four broad categories.

CORE NATIVE I (CNI)

This is someone who is born in the US and whose parents were born in the US. Heritage is known by grandparents and older generations, and there may be various cultures (not a singular culture) in the family system. The main culture is American, the main language is English, and the family doesn't regularly use a second language.

---

9   "Characteristics of the US Population by Generational Status: 2013," United States Census Bureau, accessed January 11, 2020, https://www.census.gov/library/publications/2016/demo/p23-214.html.

CORE NATIVE II (CNII)

This is someone who is born and raised in the US, but one or both of the parents is a first-generation immigrant. The parents may be from different cultures. For example, my children are Core Native II because my husband and I are both first generation (I'm from Taiwan, my husband is from Italy). People who fall under CNII may or may not speak a second language, but they know the family heritage and they might have traveled to at least one of the parents' native countries. There may have been interactions with extended family members living in one or both of the parents' home countries.

EARLY FIRST-GENERATION IMMIGRANTS (EFGI)

This is someone who moved to the US at a very young age (preschool to middle school). In these early school years, the person learns English as their second language. Depending on when they arrive in the US, they may have some of the culture and language instilled (for example, if they arrived while in sixth grade, they may already have completed early school years in their native country). EFGIs typically speak the English language with little or no accent, and they adapt well to American culture. They appear to be primarily American, but they retain some of their heritage. They may read or write in their first language to a certain degree.

LATE FIRST-GENERATION IMMIGRANTS (LFGI)

This is someone who came to the US during their later school years (high school, college, or graduate school). Most of their formal language was learned in their native country. The first language is their native language and English is a second language. The LFGI is also rooted culturally in their native country because so much of their early learning took place there. LFGIs interact with people differently than Americans do;_it may be apparent that they were not born in the US. LFGIs may travel often back to their country of origin. If applicable, they may bring their offspring—who may be CNII or EFGI—with them on trips.

As a general rule, CNI and CNII individuals should present few challenges during communication in terms of culture and language. This doesn't mean that patients from these two groups will automatically accept the treatment being proposed by the provider. There are obviously many other variants, including socioeconomic status, education level, and access to the healthcare system. These patients may very well reject the proposed treatment for reasons other than language and culture. Being a CNI or CNII simply means that there is no need for language interpreters and that we can assume individuals in this group embrace and loosely share the central core cultural beliefs called American as their primary culture.

THE GRAY AREAS

The Amalgamation Scale is not black and white; there are gray areas between the four broad categories. Do not be overly concerned about classifying a person as an EFGI or LFGI based on their entry to the US in eighth or ninth grade. Instead, look at the person's overall degree of cultural adaptation to understand the proposed treatment, whether they accept and adopt treatment based on an American standard of care or whether they preserve beliefs from their native country that are strong enough to influence their final decision-making. Sometimes there are no conflicts. For example, the belief that infection requires antibiotic treatment may be more universal and require little convincing. On the other hand, the notion of invasive surgery may be more readily accepted in certain cultures than others. Recall, from chapter two, the example of the Chinese woman with a mouth tumor who preferred to use herbal medicine over surgical treatment as an example of autorejection, a part of the Dichotomy of Treatment Trust. She fits the classic description of an LFGI.

As one can imagine, moving from EFGI to LFGI, you might encounter greater difficulty in communication, both in language and cultural values. It can be especially challenging if the healthcare provider comes from a cultural background that has very different values from the patient. That challenge can be made even more difficult when both providers are LFGI but have different communication styles. In this latter case, gender can also play a role if an LFGI patient comes from a male-dominated culture and is interacting with a female provider of a different LFGI background. The female provider might then face bias from the male patient because, in his culture, female providers may not exist or do not assume an authority role.

In the next chapter, we will further discuss the applications of the Amalgamation Scale in the context of patient care and how providers can utilize this classification to gain more knowledge in order to create a win-win situation in increasing the success of communication with patients, thereby improving treatment outcomes.

IMPROVE YOUR
Cultural Competency

1. There is an uneven distribution of diversity patterns in the US. Coastal cities are more diverse than inland cities.

2. Providers should gain understanding of how diverse their

community is and whether the challenges lie in lack of exposure to different cultural groups as a community or as an individual.

3. The Amalgamation Scale is a classification based on the age at which the individual migrates to the country and the degree of cultural adaptation based on the chronicity of being in the US.

4. The Amalgamation Scale can be used in any social or work setting to perceive ease or difficulty in interacting with people from a different cultural background than your own.

5. In the context of healthcare provider–patient relations, the Amalgamation Scale can help to gauge ease or difficulty when discussing or proposing treatment options with patients.

CHAPTER 7

Application of the Amalgamation Scale—The Value System

Human wisdom remains always one and the same
although applied to the most diverse objects and it is
no more changed by their diversity than the sunshine is
changed by the variety of objects which it illuminates.

~ **Rene Descartes**

In this chapter, I will explain how to apply the Amalgamation Scale to common examples to help facilitate better communication. To illustrate the concept, I will focus on LFGIs, or Late First-Generation Immigrants.

In chapter six, we discussed the concept of the Amalgamation Scale based on an individual's chronicity in the US, the degree of cultural adaptation that has taken place, and how much the cultural value system from their native country influences their decision-making process.

Let me first clarify: a person who has been in the US for thirty years but has been interacting within his or her own cultural community without stepping out of their comfort zone may not be as assimilated or amalgamated as someone who has lived in the US for half that time but makes a constant effort to learn and adapt to American culture. For example, when I lived and worked in the South Bronx, there were families of three generations who spoke very little English, including a grandmother who had lived in the US for more than thirty years. Their main daily interactions were mostly confined to the neighborhood in the South Bronx, and this vicinity in New York City was mostly Spanish speaking. Therefore, the length of time residing in the country is not the only determining factor in a person's cultural adaptation. Rather, if there is an immediate need for cultural adaptation, such as for work or school, then the individual is likely to have a steeper Chain of Zigzags and may present him or herself as more Americanized, as appropriate to the social or physical setting they are in.

As I mentioned before, CNI and CNII (born and raised in the US) should have little to no problem in communicating, from a language or cultural point of view. This does not mean that CNI and CNII patients will not question or refuse treatment. Other factors, such as educational level, socioeconomic factors, economic status, religious practice, political views, personal opinions, upbringing, the patient's perception, and biases and stereotypes regarding a provider's country of origin, all affect the doctor–patient relationship. These factors also affect how likely it is that a proposed treatment may be accepted by the patient as feasible.

SOCIALIZATION SHAPES BEHAVIOR: CNIIS AND EFGIS IN SCHOOL

When I was a college student at UC Berkeley, many of my friends were CNIIs and EFGIs. I belonged to a student club called Chinese

Student Union in which many members were Mandarin-speaking CNIIs and EFGIs from Taiwan and mainland China. There was also a Chinese student association in which most members were Cantonese-speaking CNIIs and EFGIs from Hong Kong. The two clubs often held joint events. Many CNIIs didn't speak Mandarin or Cantonese but had great understanding of Chinese culture. Some took Chinese classes in college and became more verbally proficient in Chinese by hanging out with their EFGI peers.

Imagine if some of these CNIIs became healthcare providers later in life. They may have had more exposure to their parents' native culture compared to CNIs and might feel better equipped and more comfortable dealing with LFGI patients because of a deeper understanding and additional layer of empathy gained from earlier social learnings.

EFGI is an interesting group because they could very well behave similarly to CNII if the individual grows up in a homogenous part of America. Many EFGIs may choose to identify more with mainstream American culture. There are many factors driving an EFGI to blend in (assimilate), including (1) earlier school experiences that left them feeling like an outsider, such as being shunned or bullied; (2) negative images of parents not speaking English or speaking with an accent and being looked down upon; and (3) cool media images of American celebrities. For example, an EFGI teenage boy might want to look like an American rapper or an NBA player that he sees on TV. They may choose to hang out with their American peers to get rid of an accent or a fresh-off-the-boat image.

On the other hand, if this EFGI lives in an area that is mostly ethnic, such as Orange County in California (which is 40 percent nonwhite, mostly Hispanic and Asian), then they may behave more like an LFGI.

The bottom line is that the Amalgamation Scale classification should be a guide to help providers predict possible barriers in communication. But beware of labeling any particular individual, because that can cause you to develop biases and stereotypes, which can affect judgment.

> *But beware of labeling any particular individual, because that can cause you to develop biases and stereotypes, which can affect judgment.*

THE AMALGAMATION SCALE APPLIED

The Amalgamation Scale can be applied to any social setting or work environment, not just in the healthcare industry. By identifying an individual as being in a particular category, we can begin to understand where potential conflicts and differences might come from based on how much cultural adaptation this person may have undergone.

Let's do an exercise. Let's apply the Amalgamation Scale to the 2018 wildly popular book-turned-movie *Crazy Rich Asians*. The main character, Rachel Chu, is a CNII who's born and raised in the US and has no accent. She identifies with American culture but also with Chinese heritage because her mother is a first-generation immigrant from China (LFGI). Rachel's boyfriend, Nick Young, is an LFGI from Singapore whose first language is English but who has a strong Singaporean-Chinese heritage from a wealthy family background. Nick is torn between old-school Chinese values and American values. Nick's mother, Eleanor, a native Singaporean-Chinese, who believes in the traditional hierarchy of the rich over the poor, perceives Rachel as being too American and low class for her son. Both Rachel's mother and Nick are LFGI, but their socioeconomic classes and countries of origin make them very different people. Clashes exist due to different sets of values that lie within different categories of the Amalgamation Scale.

Similar to the character of Nick Young from *Crazy Rich Asians*, many immigrants from other cultural backgrounds may have English as a first language or have a strong second language that is close to their mother tongue. However, cultural values are still largely a reflection of the country of origin. For example, New Jersey is one of the most diverse states in the country. In my area, there are many Indians speaking different languages, including the most commonly spoken languages in my neighborhood: Gujarati, Punjabi, Hindi, and Urdu. (The Eighth Schedule to the Constitution of India consists of twenty-two languages with demands for inclusion of thirty-eight more languages![10]) Many speak fluent English as part of their upbringing, yet they preserve traditional cultural values. Many LFGIs may arrive in the US after they have completed their higher education to seek jobs and earn middle- to upper-class incomes. Communication in terms of language is rarely an issue. Many hold very good jobs and are hard workers.

Let's revisit the example of the movie *The Farewell* from chapter four. Billie, an EFGI who spoke basic Chinese but mostly adopted American philosophy, had a hard time understanding why her family was keeping from her grandmother, Nai-Nai, her own diagnosis of terminal lung cancer. Billie constantly questioned everyone around her. She challenged the Chinese doctor, who was UK trained, and learned that even the doctor found the lie acceptable because of their

---

10   "Languages Included in the Eighth Schedule of the Indian Constitution," Government of India, Ministry of Home Affairs, Department of Official Language, accessed January 11, 2020, https://rajbhasha.gov.in/en/languages-included-eighth-schedule-indian-constitution.

culture. Billie's father, HaiYan, an LFGI who had lived in the US long enough to have adopted an American mentality, disagreed with the lie but went along with the family because "the family thinks it's better not to tell her." Both Billie and HaiYan told the family it was illegal in the US to not tell patients about their own diagnosis, but went along with the collective decision because of their cultural values. Here, you see the struggle and conflict between cultures.

Many late-first-generation patients express the wish to have treatments done in their home country. One reason is because of personal relationships. A provider in their home country may be related to the patient in some extended way ("my wife's cousin is a dentist/physician"), or it's simply that overall treatment is less expensive. Since the health system is different and the complexity of the US healthcare system is often confusing and frustrating, many times an LFGI will prefer to wait to be treated in their home country. Many LFGIs are still covered under the health system of their home country and the premium or copay may be negligible compared to the US. For frequent travelers, it may be a no-brainer to have simple procedures done in their home country because of accessibility.

For healthcare providers, the Amalgamation Scale can and should be utilized to anticipate potential communication roadblocks and to develop skills to discuss with your patients from different cultural backgrounds the differences between health systems and what the American health system can offer in terms of standard of care, specialty care, and continuity of care.

HELPING PATIENTS SEE VALUE IN THE AMERICAN HEALTHCARE SYSTEM

A colleague showed me a case where a patient had recently had multiple dental implants placed in China, and the implants were loose after just a few months. She had a long-standing history of taking antiresorptive medications for her osteoporosis. These medications are known to include risk factors for bone exposure, or osteonecrosis of the jawbone. Thus, dental surgeries, including dental implants, may not do well in patients taking antiresorptive medications. She also had periodontal diseases with bone loss, and many of her teeth were loose along with the newly placed dental implants. Removal of the teeth and/or dental implants could potentially cause jawbone exposure. My colleague also didn't know what type of dental implants were placed, nor did the patient. It is difficult to provide care in situations like this when communication becomes remote and almost impossible and the patient does not have copies of their treatment record.

When a patient tells me they prefer to receive treatments outside the US, I remind them that, if complications arise or follow-up care is required, it is difficult to maintain continuity of care between countries. This is especially true for treatments that may require multiple steps or long-term care (hip replacement, dental implants, cancer treatments, etcetera). Although the health system in the US is not without flaws, and the complexity of health insurance and continued rise in premiums often cause frustration for both patients and providers, the array of specialized doctors and availability of comprehensive care in a multidisciplinary setting can provide layers of reassurance in most cases.

The word "insurance" is misleading, because the insured is often not covered entirely. We, as healthcare providers, also need to communicate that insurance does not equal 100 percent coverage. This concept may be difficult to understand, as many parts of the world offer comprehensive care and coverage, or the treatment cost is significantly lower compared to the US. My parents used to travel back to Taiwan for dental cleanings because their copay was around $4. It was natural for my parents to receive a $4 cleaning from a dentist who had been treating them for more than twenty years. My mother-in-law in Italy was covered 100 percent for her knee replacement and rehab; however, she patiently waited three years for her surgeon to become available. That's just one example of how care is not always as readily available and convenient as one might think. For LFGIs, it is almost inevitable that they will be shopping around for doctors, hospitals, and treatments just as they would with any type of retail business, especially if they have access to healthcare systems in the US and in their native country.

I've seen a video taken on a smartphone of a street vendor in a Southeast Asian country taking out a woman's tooth with bare hands, no anesthesia, and primitive instruments. The woman passed out afterward. I recall that the last scene was zoomed in on a bloody tooth on the ground surrounded by flies. The image was vivid and repulsive.

One of my patients, a woman from Egypt, told me about how people she knew died from dental extraction procedures back home. She saw the differences in the care; she saw the value beyond the copayment, and she did not take the quality of care provided in the US for her mother for granted. In the US, it takes years of education and training to become a practitioner in any doctrine. Multiple certifications, licensing, and continuing education are required to maintain a certain level of competency. Many see the value of being treated in the US healthcare system. Others argue against it from a financial point of view. It is important to stress that, in the US, there is a vast network of providers with numerous subspecialties and different facilities, including clinics, urgent care, hospitals, assisted living, and rehab centers that can provide a continuum of comprehensive care. And third-party financing and financial aid specialists in hospitals can help patients receive the treatment they need.

OVERACCEPTANCE OF TREATMENT IN SOME LFGIS

If you have identified an LFGI patient who seems very agreeable, look for signs of overacceptance in the Dichotomy of Treatment Trust, as discussed in chapter two. Make sure to gauge the patient's language ability by asking open-ended questions. Make sure that the patient understands the documents being signed and that you discuss risks, benefits, and alternative treatments. Make sure their questions are answered. If the providers are CNI and the patient is an LFGI of a different cultural heritage, there may be more communication barriers from language and cultural standpoints. The provider then should spend more time making sure all questions are answered and understood.

Not all LFGIs are the same. In David Livermore's book, *Expand Your Borders: Discover 10 Cultural Clusters*, he explains how different "cultural clusters" exhibit different categories of characteristics. Two categories discussed, "high power distance" versus "low power distance," explain the importance of authority within these cultural clusters. For example, Confucian Asia (China, Korea, Japan, Taiwan, etcetera), Southern Asia (India, Indonesia, Malaysia, Thailand, etcetera), and Arab countries (Saudi Arabia, Egypt, Kuwait, UAE, etcetera) exhibit high power distance. These cultures in general view hierarchy as important and expect authority figures to make decisions. On the other hand, European cultures, such as Nordic (Scandinavian countries) or Anglo (Australia, the UK, the US, etcetera), usually have low power distance. Therefore, when dealing with patients from cultures with high power distance, remember that these patients may be more likely to exhibit overacceptance behavior from the Dichotomy of Treatment Trust, because authority is viewed as important. Patients from cultures of high power distance are less likely to voice doubts or complaints in the provider's presence. Providers should be conscious of the cultural differences and not dismiss the concerns or assume these patients are being passive.

"I WANT TO SEE A MALE DOCTOR"— THE PERCEIVED COMPETENCY OF FEMALE PRACTITIONERS DUE TO CULTURAL DIFFERENCES

Finally, clashes may occur if both the provider and the patient are LFGI but from very different cultural backgrounds. Very rarely have I had patients refuse to see me simply because I'm a woman. If the patient's native culture is very male-dominated, female doctors may be scarce, or if the patient has never seen a female doctor, he or she might question the competency of a female doctor. This is not directly related to the gender of the provider but to the perceived competency, simply because it's not the norm. However, if it comes to a point where the provider's credibility is greatly compromised and patient rapport cannot be properly established, it is not unreasonable to refer the patient to see a provider that he or she feels comfortable with.

IMPROVE YOUR
Cultural Competency

1. EFGIs may behave like CNIIs or LFGIs depending on their earlier socialization environment.

2. The Amalgamation Scale can be applied in any social setting or work environment. LFGIs often have access to two health systems: in the US and their native country. Financial factors often determine treatment.

3. It's important to explain to LFGIs the value of the US healthcare system, especially when continuity of care and long-term follow-ups are desired.

4. Beware of overacceptance of the Dichotomy of Treatment Trust in LFGIs.

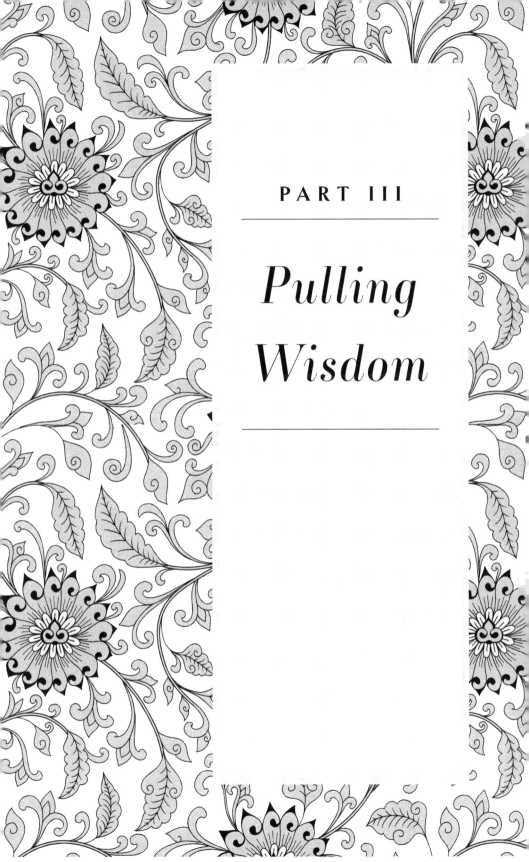

PART III

Pulling Wisdom

CHAPTER 8

Don't Yank, Pull Wisdom

Beware of false knowledge; it is more dangerous than ignorance.

~ **George Bernard Shaw**

In Tom Hanks's movie *Cast Away*, there was a scene in which his character, Chuck Noland, developed a dental infection while stranded on the island. He then proceeded to self-treat using an ice skate blade to knock out his infected tooth, along with himself. The drama created by that particular scene successfully captured the fear of dental pain and tooth extractions that many of us can relate to.

In real life, how likely is Tom Hanks's character to wake up pain free and swelling free? Almost impossible. In real life, the lack of controlled, sterile setting, DIY approach done by an untrained layman on himself, and lack of availability of antibiotics would certainly accelerate the spread of infection. Tom Hanks's character would likely wake up with a swollen face and perhaps a torn corner of lip and cut cheek from the blade—and more pain.

ATRAUMATIC EXTRACTION
TECHNIQUE EXPLAINED

When it comes to tooth extractions, many people associate them with the "tooth tied to the doorknob" or "yanking." Both of those scenarios are inaccurate portraits of reality. In actuality, the best technique that delivers nearly pain-free and swelling-free postoperative results is the atraumatic extraction technique. Contrary to popular thinking, the atraumatic extraction technique utilizes as little brute force as possible to reduce trauma to the surrounding tissue while removing a tooth. Many do not regard tooth extraction as "surgery," but it is. Techniques other than "yanking" are taught in dental school and residency to achieve optimal results. Our body regards wounds caused by trauma or surgery in a similar fashion. When a wound is inflicted on our body, a complex repair process is triggered that takes place in stages. A surgery that is done in a controlled fashion often reduces the body's inflammatory responses, which translates into less pain and swelling during the healing period.

Bear with me for a minute and allow me to explain this technique. I will help you see why this is important later in the chapter. Imagine you are a first-year dental student learning about the anatomy of a tooth. Between the tooth and the bone, there are hundreds of thousands of tiny fibers called periodontal ligaments, or PDL, connecting the tooth to the surrounding bone, holding tooth and bone together. These groups of tiny fibers connect tooth to bone in different directions, rendering them capable of withstanding significant human biting forces. To give you an idea, normal human chewing force is said to be about seventy psi (pounds per square inch), with the maximum biting force about one hundred seventy psi. That is a lot of force per bite or chewing. So, the "tie the tooth to the doorknob" technique may work in a very loose baby tooth situation where there are barely any fibers attaching the tooth to the bone, but otherwise it is not applicable for most situations.

The atraumatic tooth extraction technique, in a nutshell, involves first carefully breaking the PDL with special instruments, then moving (or luxating) the tooth with a dental instrument called the elevator in a controlled fashion to move a tooth carefully within the socket. An elevator comes in different shapes and sizes, but it resembles the gross shape of a screwdriver, although the two tools are not interchangeable. Once the tooth is loosened, another instrument, called a forceps, is used to retrieve the tooth. Most people might equate forceps with the gross shape of pliers. However, I forbid you from attempting dental extractions on anyone using common tools from Home Depot, including yourself. The purpose of this discussion is not to instruct DIY extraction technique, but to demonstrate the following concept:

Utilize the concept of atraumatic extraction technique to extract useful information in cross-cultural communication with your patients.

What do I mean by that? When treating a patient with a cultural background different from yours, it is important to approach gently with your questions, especially if you are not familiar with this patient's culture. Imagine the language and cultural barrier between you and the patient is like the PDL. You must break the barrier gently by asking the right questions and make the patient feel more comfortable with you. Once you break the initial

When treating a patient with a cultural background different from yours, it is important to approach gently with your questions, especially if you are not familiar with this patient's culture.

barrier, you can then try to communicate further about the treatment and present treatment options by moving the patient with controlled force, like using a dental elevator—be firm about why you think the treatment is necessary. Communicate with tactics. Forcing treatment by imposing your beliefs upon theirs can create discordance between you and your patient, causing more pain for both parties. Treatment not planned properly can often cause a traumatic experience for the patient later on, whether it is financial or clinical.

PULLING WISDOM

In order to build up your atraumatic extraction technique in cross-cultural doctor–patient communication, we need to pull WISDOM.

Here is the six-step WISDOM process to enhance your cross-cultural communication skills.

W **WEAVE** all the pieces of information together by asking questions. I've mentioned the importance of asking open-ended questions. Open-ended questions like these will help you to gather basic information about the patient's background and concerns:

- What is the patient's ethnicity and cultural background?

- What is the patient's religious practice that may impact the treatment? (Diet restrictions? Etiquette of male–female interactions?)

- What is the patient's perception of the healthcare system in the US? (Expensive? Complicated? Great quality of care? Comprehensive?)

- What is the patient's main concern about the treatment? (Is it the interpreter's availability? Is it finances?)

I INITIATE conversations. Once you have asked questions to gather basic information about a patient, try to connect to the patient by having short, simple conversations. Throughout the book, I have used examples of food as a connector. If you are experienced with multicultural flair in your personal life, such as through traveling experiences, this should come more easily to you in helping you strike up a conversation. Nonthreatening, common topics that serve as lower common denominators are typically good.

Examples of questions generating an opening conversation with a patient from Turkey:

- How long does it take to travel from Turkey to the US?

- What is the typical weather there?

- What is a good season to travel?

- Are there any taboos there that travelers should know? I am thinking about visiting.

- What are the popular dishes over there?

- Do you know any local restaurants that serve Turkish food?

- Do you find it very different here in the US? In what ways?

Asking questions about geography, customs, and food typically are good starters. Avoid using slang. Use simple words. Saying "sign your name here" is more easily understood than "I need your John Hancock here." American humor is quite different and may not be well understood by someone who is still learning English. Popular culture and trivia may not be well understood either. Speak slowly and sincerely.

S CULTURAL SENSITIVITY. Using guidelines from the last chapter, avoid "you are all the same" conversations to refer to a culture similar to the patient's. Always ask if you are not sure. Avoid assumptions.

Questions to a Chinese person such as "So what do you think about eating dog meat?" are extremely insulting and show a lack of sensitivity or knowledge about another culture.

In many Asian countries, such as China, Japan, Korea, or Vietnam, a person's family name comes first. Most of the time, American or English translations with alphabetical spellings distort the original names. South Asian names and Eastern European names can be very long with multiple syllables. Ask patients how they pronounce their name or how they would like to be addressed. Do not mock. Many might choose to adopt American names, like myself, as they are commonly accepted. Address patients how they want to be addressed, with whichever name they prefer.

In many cultures, seniority plays a major role. Therefore, it is always a good idea to address your patients as Mr., Miss, or Mrs. plus their last name, rather than using their first name, especially if the patient is older. Formality creates an instant sense of respect and is encouraged in doctor–patient interactions.

If you work in an area that has a certain ethnic affinity, it is not a bad idea to do research on your own about the customs, including dietary restrictions, holidays, and cultural or religious beliefs about that particular ethnic group. When I was an oral surgery attending at a local hospital in Lakewood, New Jersey, an area with a high Orthodox Jewish population, I received an information packet from the hospital outlining Jewish customs and cultural etiquette regarding the Sabbath, using separate hospital elevators, and other customs I was not familiar with. Nowadays, internet research is at your fingertips. I encourage you to research your patients' customs. This is a win-win situation to make yourself more educated and to make communication with your patient easier.

DECODE nonverbal cues/body language. Nonverbal cues are almost universal and can be more important than verbal communication. If you walk into a room and the patient is looking at you with arms and legs crossed, or pulling away at your touch, you can probably detect that this patient is in a defensive mode, most likely due to fear either because of bad past experiences or fear of the unknown. Somatic fight-and-flight responses such as raspy breathing, shaking, pale skin, racing heartbeat, withdrawing, facial grimaces, or even weeping can all give you clues that the patient is afraid. It is important to immediately establish with the patient, with or without an interpreter, that "we are just talking." Ask the patient to take a deep breath with you and relax. Sit right at a patient's eye level, rather than standing, which can appear more intimidating. Pull your chair closer to converse with the patient and speak in a calm, even, slow manner regardless of whether the patient can fully understand you or not. Direct eye contact is important to show that you are sincere and serious about your conversation. Sometimes in such a situation, I may lightly pat the patient's shoulder or forearm, which I consider socially acceptable safe zones for body contact. If you are a male practitioner, you may offer a handshake, as some other form of physical contact may not be perceived as acceptable between males and females in other cultures.

I remember when my Taiwanese parents were about to meet with my Roman sister-in-law. My sister-in-law was warned by my husband not to do the kiss-on-the-cheek thing. In spite of the warning, my sister-in-law went to hug and kiss both of my parents on the cheek. My father froze on the spot and looked uncomfortable and embarrassed. It was similar to the scene from the movie *My Big Fat Greek Wedding* when both sets of parents met. We laughed it off afterward, but in my culture, we don't kiss on the cheek. Men and women, when they first meet, usually nod politely as acknowledgment. Handshakes are permissible, but other forms of body contact are usually not invited. If you are from a Latin culture and your patient is from an East Asian, Southeast Asian, or Middle Eastern culture, be aware of body contact in the social context. Don't blow it off and try to justify the behavior as, "Oh, this is just the way we [cultural background] are because we are passionate." Respect the other's cultural customs. When in doubt, it is always better to be formal than informal.

When x-rays are taken in my office, we ask patients to remove any jewelry that could potentially show up on the x-ray to create artifacts. That includes earrings, tongue rings, lip rings, nose rings, and also hair pins or clips for the head wrap. It is important to create a safe environment for female Muslim patients to remove their head wrap, or hijab, in order to facilitate taking the imaging. Communicate ahead of time what your expectations are with the patient so that there is no misunderstanding.

Dr. Farah Roslan, while a student at University Hospitals of Derby and Burton NHS Trust, created what may be the first disposable hijab to be used by staff in the hospital.[11] This is applaudable and one step closer to providing comfort and convenience for female doctors of the Muslim religion.

O OFFER OPTIONS AND RESOURCES. With even basic knowledge you gain about your patients' backgrounds

---

11 "Royal Derby Hospital: Disposable Sterile Hijabs Introduced," *BBC News*, accessed January 11, 2020, https://www.bbc.com/news/uk-england-derbyshire-50810176.

through conversations or your research, it can become helpful, especially in an outpatient setting, to offer options and resources. For example, a Muslim patient of mine came to me to schedule a procedure during Ramadan, which consists of one month of strict daily fasting from four o'clock in the morning to eight o'clock at night. Since I typically recommend patients keep up with their calorie intake after their mouth surgery procedure, I explained about the recovery course and recommended that he return after Ramadan for his elective procedure. I wanted to make sure he had enough nutrition during his healing period. At the end of the discussion, he was very pleased, because he didn't expect an Asian to know about his customs. He happily told my front desk on the way out of the office, "This doctor knows me!" When he returned for his treatment, he was grinning from ear to ear and told me he trusted me to do his procedure. Similarly, when a patient has limited language proficiency and refuses to be referred out to another specialist simply because of a language issue, it is important for the provider to direct the patient to a facility where interpretation is available.

MONEY FACTOR. As you may recall from chapter two, I talked about autorejection in the Dichotomy of Treatment Trust, where patients may automatically reject treatments due to copay issues. In chapter seven, I also pointed out that many LFGIs may have access to the US health system as well as a health system back home. When there is resistance from the patients due to money, is it an issue of seeing the value of the treatment or of the sheer dollar amount of the treatment?

In other words, patients may be unwilling to pay for a $50 consultation. In their eyes, consultations may not offer value because "nothing was done" and "we were just talking." As a practitioner, I consider the initial consultation the most important encounter with the patient. During the consultation, the patient's medical history is reviewed and a clinical examination is performed. This is also the time to utilize the Amalgamation Scale to gauge possible roadblocks in further communication and anticipate concerns or questions that may arise due to cultural differences. I emphasize the importance of a consultation with the patient because, aside from the clinical assessment, the initial consultation helps to develop rapport with the patient. The value of a consultation is far greater than $50.

On the other hand, patients may not go forward with the treatment simply because the treatment fee is a high dollar amount, especially when compared to what is offered in their home country. Providers may offer third-party financing options if credit has been established in the US. It is important that providers discuss with patients the pros and cons of receiving treatment in the US versus returning to their home country. Providers need to discuss the value of continuity of care, standard of care, the availability of FDA-approved medications and services, along with the wide array of specialists providing services and accessibility of providers. When I visited Italy years ago, my child was infected with conjunctivitis. Similar to Asia, medications such as antibiotics or eye drops can be sold at a local pharmacy in Italy. The only thing was that the closest two pharmacies were both closed for one month with notices on the doors stating that the owner went on vacation in the summer months. There were no corporate drug stores such as CVS or Rite Aid, so we drove around until we finally found a pharmacy one hour away. In the US, it is unlikely that any pharmacy would be closed for one month due to the owner taking vacation, but in Italy, the inconvenience is an acceptable part of the culture.

In the next chapter, I will elaborate on teaching your team to increase cultural competency. Most of the time, your team members will be the first to engage with your patients—even before you meet with your patients. Therefore, it is especially important to train your team members to raise their cultural sensitivity and increase their level of cultural competency when dealing with patient care.

IMPROVE YOUR
Cultural Competency

1. The atraumatic extraction technique should be used to extract important information during patient encounters. Carefully break down the barriers and approach gently. Do not impose.

2. Learn how to pull WISDOM in order to build up the atraumatic extraction technique.

3. Pulling WISDOM consists of the following six steps: Weave all the information together, Initiate conversations, develop cultural Sensitivity, Decode nonverbal cues or body language, Offer options and resources, and discuss the Money factor.

CHAPTER 9

Team Development Equals Success Conversion

A chain is only as strong as its weakest link.

~ English Proverb

When I was a resident, this story was circulating: A surgeon was operating with an Indian scrub nurse. He was frustrated with her because she was making too many mistakes and, in his view, was moving too slowly when handing him the proper surgical instruments. In response, he would press on her bindi (the red dot on her forehead) repeatedly while saying, "Reset, reset, reset!"

While I didn't know whether the story was fictitious or true, or whether this surgeon was disciplined, I knew that behavior was extremely offensive. Insensitive comments or actions made in work situations are often dismissed due to a couple of reasons. One is that a supervisor who is not culturally aware or sensitive to other cultures calls the shots, and therefore gets away with making insensitive comments to subordinates. The other is that the team is relatively homogenous and unaware of other cultural values. Therefore, when comments and actions that are offensive to members of a minority (not necessarily in the sense of race but of the cultural makeup of the team) are made, complaints against those comments are often dismissed because the team doesn't think it's a big deal.

THE NEGATIVE IMPACT OF STEREOTYPES

Dr. Chad Gehani, current president of the American Dental Association, is a first-generation immigrant from India. He told me a story when I visited him in his Chicago office.

He was invited to speak at a conference. Before speaking, however, he was sitting in the audience when a woman questioned what nationality he was. Dr. Gehani replied, "I am an American, made in India." Imagine the woman's surprise when Dr. Gehani then walked up to speak as the president of the ADA, a role that has predominantly been filled by Caucasian men in the past.

Misconceptions often stem from stereotypes, which in turn generate negative emotions. Steele and Aronson, in their 1995 landmark article, "Stereotype and the Intellectual Test through Performance of African Americans," conducted an experiment that resulted in the term "stereotype threat," which is defined as "being at risk of confirming, as self-characteristic, a negative stereotype about one's group."[12] In this study, black and white students were given a difficult test, the Graduate Record Examination. Half of the students were told that it was a diagnostic intelligence test and half were not. Interestingly, black students performed worse when compared to white students when told that it was a diagnostic intelligence test, but they performed equally as well as white students when they were told

---

12   C.M. Steele and J. Aronson, "Stereotype and the Intellectual Test through Performance of African Americans," *Journal of Personality and Social Psychology* 69, no. 5 (1995): 797–811.

that it was a nondiagnostic test of intelligence. The study postulated that stereotypes activate self-doubt, trigger anxiety, and negatively impact an individual's performance related to intellectual ability.

Burgess and associates, in the article "Stereotype Threat and Health Disparities: What Medical Educators and Future Physicians Need to Know," further elaborated on the consequences when patients are under stereotype threat.[13] The article points out that patients are more likely to become noncompliant and less communicative and to discount advice or even avoid physicians who make them feel inferior. Patients also disidentify themselves from what are considered "white" behaviors, such as exercising, eating healthy, and reinforcing stereotypes.

In other words, if patients perceive healthcare providers as being biased and judgmental based on cultural stereotypes, it is more likely that patients may have a negative experience and disengage from interactions with providers.

In earlier chapters, I explained the Dichotomy of Treatment Trust of overacceptance and autorejection to describe different patient behavior stemming from different cultural beliefs. I described the Amalgamation Scale to show you the process of socialization to a new culture depending on when the individual lands in this country. In the last chapter, I also suggested utilizing the atraumatic extraction technique to pull WISDOM in order to enhance your communication with your patients.

By now, you, as a healthcare provider, have gained more awareness and knowledge about how to understand patients with different cultural backgrounds and spoken languages and how to

---

13   DJ Burgess, J. Warren, S. Phelan, J. Dovidio, and M. van Ryn, "Stereotype Threat and Health Disparities: What Medical Educators and Future Physicians Need to Know," *The Journal of General Internal Medicine*, suppl 2: S169-77 (May 2010), doi: 10.1007/s11606-009-1221-4.

improve your communication with them. However, oftentimes, your team members are the ones who have the first encounters with patients. Your staff members may be of a different cultural background than you, other staff members, or your patients. It is possible to have disagreements or conflicts within your own team due to cultural differences. There might also be misunderstandings in communication between team members and patients, either over the phone or in person. Oftentimes, team development focuses on practice profitability and work performance without addressing diversity and inclusion. As America becomes more diverse by the day, cultural competency should become a routine part of staff training. Hiring a team with a diverse background is only the beginning. Hiring team members of different nationalities and cultural backgrounds does not automatically equate to cultural competency. Not knowing how to communicate internally within the team and externally with patients due to lack of cultural sensitivity and understanding can cause discordance and a decrease in work performance and job satisfaction, and ultimately impede practice success.

Therefore, team development of cultural competency should have two components. Internal team development emphasizes how team members of different cultural backgrounds can understand and get along with one another better, and external team development focuses on raising awareness of different cultural values and welcoming people of different backgrounds in your practice. Internal and external development go hand in hand when developing a successful practice. Now let's look at some of the ways to do just that.

Internal and external development go hand in hand when developing a successful practice.

INCORPORATE TEAM DEVELOPMENT IN YOUR PRACTICE

When I graduated from my oral surgery residency in 2004, I started working in a Jewish practice in South New Jersey. Without knowing too much about Jewish culture, I was readily embraced and welcomed as a new doctor. I liked that we didn't work Saturdays and finished the day early due to sundown, and I enjoyed having days off on Jewish holidays such as Yom Kippur and Rosh Hashanah. The practice was kind to its doctors. We got to use our own patient forms and we chose our own operatory, our personal assistants, and of course, our coffee pods for the Keurig coffee machine.

One time, when I was asked which flavor pod I wanted to order, I said without hesitation, "German Chocolate Cake." I had tried that flavor recently and loved it. There was a pause, a silence. And then German Chocolate Cake was ordered (though never reordered).

When I looked back at that small incident, which I was certain no one would ever recall, it was an innocent, ignorant episode that most likely bore no significance of any kind. But there are other times when innocent comments can be offensive. When my father once visited me at work, one of my assistants referred to him as "the little guy." My father was five-foot-seven, thus "little" by American male standards. In general, I recommend against using descriptives that refer to physical size, such as "little," "tiny," or "skinny," because these often have embedded derogatory connotations associated with weakness and reinforce negative cultural stereotypes. Most people are careful to avoid language such as "large," but the opposite is just as insensitive.

For organizations or practice owners, I recommend including the following in your periodic staff training sessions.

Utilize the WISDOM principles when training your team, emphasizing:

- Identify the demographics of your team members. Do you work in a diverse or homogeneous environment? Is one member of the team "outed" compared to the rest? For example, is your team mostly comprised of blondes with one or two minority team members?

- What are the current issues within the work environment? Do some members of your team appear to be quieter and not as integrated into the team in work and social situations? Do some members of your team tend to talk over others?

- Are there any communication issues due to language proficiency? Accents? Members being made fun of because of their accents? Members' feelings being dismissed after they are made fun of ("Oh relax, it's just a joke")?

Periodic staff meetings should include a cultural segment. For example, members of different cultural backgrounds are encouraged to share fun facts about their cultural traditions in meetings to educate other members. If there was an incident or situation with patients of a different background, staff meetings should allow opportunities to discuss.

Hold workshops with questionnaires to gain employee feedback on culturally related behavior so that other employees understand the best strategies for relating to those from other cultures. For example, "I dislike it when someone uses the word 'Oriental girl' when describing me."

Discuss different communication styles during team meetings. Some cultures that communicate in a very direct manner, or which are very inquisitive in their communications, can be interpreted as being pushy or rude, while other cultures communicate in an indirect manner, where "maybe" or "yes" can mean "no." When communicating with people from cultures that have a direct communication style, keep conversations brief and direct as well. When communicating with people from cultures that are more indirect in nature, make sure to hold follow-up calls after patients leave. Some patients will avoid confrontation in person and will be more direct over the phone. Discussing stereotypes with your staff and consequences of stereotypes will affect your relationship with your patients.

Cultural appreciation events or ethnic holiday celebration for members, where discussion of traditions can be held and ethnic food can be shared. One year, I was invited to my Persian dentist friend's office to celebrate Nowruz, the Iranian festival of spring. All staff members and other doctors were also invited. I brought her hydrangea flowers and we had fruits, nuts, and confectionaries, including chickpea cookies with rose water (nan-e nokhodchi). She explained Persian traditions and celebration rituals. I thought it was delightful as well as educational.

Cultural expertise of staff. If you have a bilingual or multilingual staff member who is proficient in medical terminology and can work as an efficient translator, consider yourself very lucky. Medical and dental staff who are proficient in not only languages but who also communicate with confidence on your behalf can be very helpful in building up patients' trust quickly.

Give out packets of information about cultural traditions and customs of a particular ethnic group you serve in your practice. As I mentioned in a previous chapter, when I went onboard as an attending with a local community hospital that served a large population of Orthodox Jewish patients, I was given an information packet about the customs and traditions of Jewish culture. I found that packet very considerate and educational. If your local communities have a certain cultural affinity, I would suggest that you research the customs and traditions of that particular community.

I remember one time I walked into Stop & Shop, a local supermarket, during the Lunar New Year. I was looking for daffodil plants, a traditional plant for the Chinese New Year. The friendly florist pointed out to me that there were some flower bouquets made by a particular company for Chinese New Year celebration. What I found was a mixed bouquet wrapped in red paper with some auspicious Chinese characters printed on the wrapping. There were many of those bouquets sitting on the shelf, starting to wither. I looked around, found no daffodils, thanked the clerk, and walked away. I thought, *These bouquets would never be sold to a Chinese person, or rather an Asian person.* They were mixed bouquets of red roses, baby's breath, and yellow chrysanthemums. Yellow and white chrysanthemums are considered funeral flowers in Chinese culture. No one would buy funeral flowers as a gift for anyone unless they were attending a funeral. Typically, small orange trees or daffodils are New Year's plants. Unfortunately, this company did not do its research on the culture of its target market, and hence was left with wasted fresh flowers that could be sold for other purposes.

Open-door policy to discuss cultural conflicts in your practice. Be prepared for there to be situations that could arise due to cultural differences among your team. In team meetings, team members from certain cultures may not necessarily raise hands to ask questions because, in their culture, that may be considered intrusive or viewed as creating conflict. In situations where conflict resolution is needed, it may not be a bad idea to approach individuals and speak to them privately.

Awareness is the first step to success. Train your team to understand the broad differences between cultural groups. These are some of the examples I discuss with my team members:

- Be aware of the importance of personal distance (generally no touching in the forms of kissing and hugging during the first meeting) in Asian and Middle Eastern cultures. Avoid hand gesturing because of assumed lack of language proficiency. In a previous chapter, I gave the example of removing a head wrap before taking an x-ray. Your team member should approach the patient and say, "In order to take a good quality x-ray, we will need you to remove your head wrap and remove all the hair pins as well as the earrings so that they don't show on the x-ray. There is no one else around, would you feel comfortable removing the head wrap right now?"

- Asian cultures do not call someone who is more senior by their first name, especially when there is no relationship established. When in doubt, go formal. It is always better to address someone as Mr., Miss, or Mrs., rather than by first name only.

- Do not hand gesture at someone because of assumed lack of language proficiency. In my earlier days living in the US, I was hand gestured at several times because of the ethnic name on my Taiwanese passport. People assumed I didn't speak English, and I felt like I was being summoned like a pet. Talk to patients like you would to your other English-speaking patients. Look into their eyes, smile, speak slowly. Use open-hand, palm-side-up gestures to show them where they should go, rather than waving your index fingers at your patients. Unfortunately, I still see this gesture a lot at the airport when going through security and customs.

- In general, financial treatment plans are better discussed in a discreet manner, whether it is with a lower tone of voice or in a separate room. In many cultures, the inability to pay is considered a shame and the person who is financially responsible for the adult patient can be an authority figure of the household, oftentimes the father or the husband. Also, in many cultures, the authority figure of the family may insist on accompanying the patient through every single step, even during the treatment. It is viewed as a protective gesture in certain cultures; however, it can seem a nuisance to providers. Understand where it is coming from and reassure the patient's family that the patient will be treated in a safe manner by professionals.

- If you use multilingual instructions, inject cultural components into your instructions to make patients understand better. For example, I have postoperative instructions in a simplified version of Chinese (used in mainland China), traditional version of Chinese (used in Taiwan and Hong Kong), and English. My African American assistant knows to ask me "simplified or traditional?" when giving patients instructions based on their written language of preference. In my post-op instructions, there is a list of food that is suggested for postoperative purposes. My soft food list in English is different from the Chinese ones. I have porridge and tofu on my Chinese soft food list as compared to Jell-O, pudding, and mashed potatoes. This is not to say Chinese people don't eat mashed potatoes, but it is easier for patients to adhere to a list of items that they are familiar with.

TEAM SUCCESS EQUALS PRACTICE SUCCESS

Having a team that is culturally competent can increase positivity in the practice and promote a more communicative atmosphere. Once you and your team establish rapport with patients who are of a different background from your own, subsequent visits will go smoother. Bond with your team members and patients through common topics that are not threatening; ask open-ended questions; educate yourself by reading books, watching programs, attending cultural events, and making friends of different nationalities and origins; and travel whenever possible. Be careful of labeling someone with stereotypes. Avoid mockery.

Whether you are a provider who was born and raised in the US trying to learn about other cultures or a provider not born and raised in the US but who is trying to learn about mainstream American culture as well as other cultures, let cultural awareness be the first step in the journey of cultural competency. Only acknowledgment of our blind spots can put us on a path to improving what we don't know.

IMPROVE YOUR
Cultural Competency

1. Stereotypes cause negative impact to patient care.

2. Team development has two components, external and internal. Both should be incorporated in periodic staff training.

3. Utilize the WISDOM principle for office team training with specific emphasis on raising awareness and increasing communication within the team and with patients.

4. Continue to pull WISDOM from individuals of different cultural backgrounds.

CHAPTER 10

The "Too" Syndrome—If You Are a Female, Minority Doctor

None of us can know what we are capable of until we are tested.

~ **Elizabeth Blackwell**

When I was in my surgical residency in the Bronx, around the early 2000s, the hospital calls in my program were divided in such a way that oral surgery residents shared rotating in-house calls with general dentistry residents. Oral surgery residents would supervise general dentistry residents in handling emergency calls overnight. My program was a Level I trauma center. My pager would often go off nonstop throughout the night—all night.

In our general dentistry department, there was an ex-cop turned dentist who looked older and more respectable than his actual age. He even had silver hair in his mustache. When we learned about ballistics of gunshot wounds, he would bring casings of different bullets to show. He was a man of few words with a smile on his face, and was well liked by the guys. I didn't know him well, but we remained friendly.

One night, we were on call together and handled some emergencies back to back. At the conclusion of the overnight call, he said to me in admiration, "You were a beast in the ER. *I thought you were just some pretty face.*"

I didn't say anything back to him, as I was still digesting his words, but I was stunned. As he gained respect for me that night, I lost respect for him because of the comment he made.

The first few years in my practice, I was still somewhat struggling being a muted alien. Looking younger at that time, I often received comments such as "How long have you been in practice?" "Have you done this before?" "Are you strong enough to take out a tooth?" "Can I see a male doctor?" When I first opened my practice, I purchased some equipment. During the transaction, I asked the company representative questions about my options for different kinds of equipment setups. He smirked at me and said, "Why don't you go home and ask your husband first?" Later, I heard that he was terminated by his company due to various instances of inappropriate comments made toward female doctors.

One time, I visited another specialist's office. He was an older gentleman. He greeted me and complimented me on my look, saying, "You know, you could pass for a trophy wife." He might have thought I would be flattered. I was not.

Jamie Katuna, a third-year medical student in California and an athlete and blogger, described similar experiences in her January 2018 blog, "'You're Too Small to Be a Surgeon' and Other Things Women in Medicine Hear." She described how she "took care of an older man in the ER and he told me straight to my face: shouldn't you be home in the kitchen?"[14]

---

14   "'You're Too Small to Be a Surgeon' and Other Things Women in Medicine Hear," Jamie Katuna, January 2018, https://www.jamiekatuna.com/blogs/2018/1/3/youre-too-small-to-be-a-surgeon-and-other-things-women-in-medicine-hear.

In my recent interactions with many female practitioners, I discovered that this same music keeps on playing over and over again. The question of whether female practitioners of various different cultural backgrounds are as competent as their male counterparts remains a topic in discussion groups. This problem is especially accentuated if the female practitioner is young. I recently wrote an article for the American Dental Association's *New Dentist Now* blog titled "You Look Too Young to Be a Dentist" to discuss the perceptions of patients and recommendations for new dentists to establish authority with patients.[15]

THE "TOO" SYNDROME OF WOMEN PRACTITIONERS

Are female practitioners, especially those who are of different cultural backgrounds, good enough in the public's eyes? Do we suffer from "Too" Syndrome? Are we:

- too young?
- too little/too big?
- too short/too tall?
- too fair/too dark?
- too pretty/sexy/attractive?
- wearing skirts too short?
- wearing necklines too low?
- too exotic?

---

15 "You look too young to be a dentist," Cathy Hung, January 2020, https://newdentistblog.ada.org/you-look-too-young-to-be-a-dentist/.

- too soft?

- too nice?

- too aggressive?

- too cold?

- too passive?

- talking too low, or too high-pitched?

- too "non-doctor-looking"?

Are we still being perceived with the "Too" Syndrome, even if we do not carry ourselves as such?

In my participation with many discussion groups, many female doctors express that we are often assumed to be non-doctor personnel or the doctors' spouses by patients at trade shows and conferences, even if our coats, scrubs, and badges clearly state "doctor."

Additional challenges can arise with patients from countries where female practitioners are scarce or if patients have never been treated by women practitioners. The occupation-related gender biases and stereotypes pose additional difficulty when female doctors try to establish rapport, credibility, and referrals from patients and other doctors.

If you are a female practitioner, and/or of a minority culture— you might dress differently, you might have an accent, or you may not look like a typical "Dr. McDreamy"—what might be the best strategies to establish yourself as an expert in your patients' eyes?

According to the Association of American Medical Colleges (AAMC), in 2019, for the first time, the majority of medical students were women: 50.5 percent of all medical school students. There is also an increase in minority applicants: a 6.3 percent increase in those of Hispanic, Latino, or Spanish origin; a 3.2 percent increase in black or

African American applicants; and 5.5 percent increase in American Indian or Alaska Native new enrollees.[16] According to the American Dental Association's data, in 2018–2019, 50.5 percent of predoctoral dental students were also female.[17] In *Dental Economics* magazine's May 2017 article, "The Shifting Paradigm of Dentistry: The Predominance of Women," author Stephanie Needham stated that "the phenomenon is global." She pointed out that women account for more than 60 percent of all practicing dentists in Europe. She also pointed out that women accounted for 50–60 percent of dental school students in India.[18] These data show a shift in the paradigm of our workforce from male to female, a shift that is expected to continue.

In light of this shift, I recommend communicating with your patients about the change in today's workforce in the United States and around the world. Educate your patients that there are as many women as men doctors or dentists in the workforce today and it is predicted that women may

> *Educate your patients that there are as many women as men doctors or dentists in the workforce today and it is predicted that women may outnumber men in the future.*

16 "The Majority of US Medical Students Are Women, New Data Show," Association of American Medical Colleges, 2019, https://www.aamc.org/news-insights/press-releases/majority-us-medical-students-are-women-new-data-show.

17 "How Many Dental Schools Are There in the US and Canada?" American Dental Association, 2018-19 Survey of Dental Education, Report 1: Academic Programs, Enrollment, and Graduates, accessed December 15, 2019, https://www.ada.org/en/science-research/health-policy-institute/dental-statistics/education.

18 Stephanie Needham, "The Shifting Paradigm of Dentistry: The Predominance of Women," *Dental Economics* (2017), https://www.dentaleconomics.com/macro-op-ed/article/16389709/the-shifting-paradigm-of-dentistry-the-predominance-of-women.

outnumber men in the future. Talk to them about the years of education and training you must go through in order to be in a position to treat them.

Thank your patients for paying you a compliment for your youthful look. Reassure them that you have received enough schooling and experience to treat patients. Say with a professional tone of voice, "I assure you that you are in good hands and I will take care of your problems." I respectfully declined a patient's wish to squeeze my arm muscles because she wanted to know if I was strong enough to take out a tooth. I must explain that techniques are involved in performing a procedure, and not brute force. With these extra measures, hopefully it will become rarer for a patient to demand to see a male doctor because of his or her own biases. Certainly, however, if a situation becomes too uncomfortable and rapport cannot be established, you may choose to refer to another colleague.

Display your credentials in the office and on your website. In this day and age, many offices have social media and many practitioners choose to post video blogs, share patient testimonials, or set up YouTube channels to introduce their practice. These may be good ways to establish rapport before meeting with your patients.

I also recommend that companies and organizations attempt to educate their employees on the changing workforce in medicine and dentistry at trade shows. It is important that organizations are being educated on diversity and inclusion in our professions, to raise awareness of cultural sensitivity. Know that there are many female clinicians who may come from different cultural backgrounds, who are different physical sizes, or who may talk in a low voice or with an accent. But none of those aspects of who they are should take away from their credentials. Educate company reps to address female doctors as doctors, not by first name, no matter how young they might look. Addressing them professionally reflects more favorably on the image of the company.

Bridging the gap across cultures certainly needs effort from both parties—the healthcare provider and the patient. Educating patients to make them understand the changing demographics of our profession is an important step to more acceptance of a doctor outside the stereotypical image of an older, white male.

If you are a woman doctor, keep your head high and communicate with confidence. State the facts, avoid knee-jerk reactions, and don't self-doubt. Defuse an embarrassing or unpleasant conversation however you choose—with humor, professionalism, and tactics. Continue to provide excellent care, because that is the only thing that will prevail and eventually break the barrier.

IMPROVE YOUR
Cultural Competency

1. The "Too" Syndrome appears to be common for female practitioners.

2. Educate your patients about the changing demographics in the healthcare profession and about your training and credentials.

3. Trade companies should consider cultural competency training to raise awareness on the shifting paradigm of female practitioners in the industry.

4. Female doctors are encouraged to continue communicating with confidence.

Conclusion

Cultural competency for healthcare professionals starts with awareness. The very first encounter with your patient may begin the second your patient calls your office. The patient may speak with an accent that you or your staff members don't quite understand. It might take much longer to gather basic information from someone who was not born and raised in the US due to the language barrier. It might be a fourteen-year-old daughter who speaks perfect English calling for her father who doesn't. These patients may need more time to fill out patient forms in your office; they might be hesitant or refuse to sign paperwork because they don't understand why it is necessary to do so. You may need to allow much more time to conduct a consultation when translation is needed. Providers have an active role in bridging the gaps in communication.

The Chain of Zigzags, or my theory of second-language acquisition, explains how each person acquires second-language skills such as reading, writing, speaking, and comprehension differently, depending on whether there is an immediate need for improvement in such skills, such as that required by school or work. Providers should develop a keen sense to detect whether a patient whose native tongue is not English truly comprehends what's being conveyed by asking direct, open-ended questions in simple English.

The two responses from the Dichotomy of Treatment Trust, overacceptance and autorejection, may occur due to differences in cultural beliefs. When the patient is overly agreeable, be sure that they understand all risks, benefits, and alternatives involved in the proposed treatment. When the patient rejects your treatment automatically, find out why and whether this has to do with conflicting cultural beliefs. Offer options and alternatives, even second opinions, so that questions will be answered. Communication styles can be largely cultural. In cultures that communicate less directly, such as East Asian cultures, patients may not confront practitioners to avoid disrespect or conflict. Taking additional steps to follow up after your initial conversation may be a good idea to find out if the patient was just trying to save face by being nice.

Interpreters have an active role, and the objectivity of translated content can be explained by the Objectivity-Subjectivity Gradient. In general, when interpreters are also financially responsible for the patient, interpretation becomes more subjective and the discussion can largely depend upon the interpreter. Medical personnel who also serve as interpreters can be very beneficial in establishing rapport with the patient. Many hospitals employ video interpretation machines that serve as helpful means by allowing simultaneous communication to occur. Machine interpreters, such as Google Translate, can still cause errors in terms of context but they eliminate human bias. When in doubt, some interpretation is still better than no interpretation.

HIPAA rules need to be kept in mind when communicating with patients whose English proficiency is in question and who require an interpreter. Make sure the interpreter is someone the patient identifies as being permitted to relay information. All HIPAA general rules apply when interpretation is required. Refer to HHS.gov for more information.

Staying within a cultural niche is common in the network of referrals. It is certainly possible to break the cultural barrier, but work needs to be done. Providers need to extend themselves by conducting research to help them understand the demographics they serve in the community and to build rapport with patients through nonthreatening topics, such as food, customs, or travel experience.

> *Providers need to extend themselves by conducting research to help them understand the demographics they serve in the community and to build rapport with patients through nonthreatening topics, such as food, customs, or travel experience.*

Learn about the Amalgamation Scale, which is a classification system based on the age and time period at which the individual migrates to the country. This will help to identify individuals whose cultural beliefs are strong and may present roadblocks in communication, especially when cultural core beliefs may be conflicting. LFGIs typically are more rooted in their native cultural beliefs. Conflicts in communication may arise if LFGIs belong to very different cultures in terms of communication style. Expect to see the Dichotomy of Treatment Trust in some cases.

When it comes to extracting useful information from your patients, employ the atraumatic extraction technique by approaching patients gently and tactfully. Utilize the principles of WISDOM:

W Weave all the pieces of information together by asking open-ended questions.

I Initiate conversations with your patients.

S cultural Sensitivity should be developed. Avoid "you're all the same" comments.

D Decode nonverbal cues and body language.

O Offer alternatives to and resources about your proposed treatment.

M Money factor. Explain the value system so that your patients will understand the differences between health systems in the US and those of their native country. Oftentimes, patients have access to both systems.

Team development is as important as your individual development. Team members are often the first ones to encounter your patients. Utilize the same principles mentioned above and incorporate them into your staff training sessions in order to raise cultural awareness. Better communication will translate into better patient retention and therefore practice success. Avoid stereotypes and learn how to communicate with different cultural styles.

If you are a female and minority doctor, you might encounter different perceptions from your peers or patients. It is important to educate your patients about the shifting paradigm in the medical and dental professions. Use humor, professionalism, and tactics to better your communication with your patients. Trade shows and companies are encouraged to provide cultural competency training for their employees in order to break through the stereotypes of white, male doctors.

Continuing to pull WISDOM from your patients using the concepts and techniques shown in this book can largely improve your provider–patient relationship. Getting your team to participate in cultural events that are entertaining and educational are great ways to elevate your practice.

DIVERSITY AND INCLUSION IN AMERICA

Thirty years ago, if you were to interview my younger self about what I envisioned myself doing when I moved to the United States, the last thing I would have said was "write a book on cultural competency for healthcare professionals." Arriving on a student visa in 1991, I migrated from the West Coast to the East Coast and now reside in New Jersey, which I call home.

I am grateful for how my life choices, although they seemed coincidental at the time, planted me purposefully and meaning-fully on different parts of the American map and equipped me with current practices to serve the people of America through schooling, training, and working in different cultural settings. I never intention-ally sought out this way. I went where my visa led me.

However, years into practice, when more patients started to tell me I made them feel more comfortable, that I eased their anxiety, I realized that it was because I was becoming more comfortable around American people. At some point, I had unknowingly broken through the perpetual outsideness of immigrants. Patients are now more comfortable with me because I am more comfortable with myself as an American provider.

Still, I want to remember where I came from and what I went through, and I want to continue to learn the ever-evolving amalgamated culture of America. Diversity and inclusion are real parts of American culture embedded in schools and workplaces, including corporations, government, military, and the healthcare system. I hope that together, we can all learn to pull WISDOM from someone who may look or live drastically differently from us and simply learn without prejudice. It is only then that you will cross language barriers and cease to see colors.

I would like to conclude this book with a lesson from Confucius:

> Wisdom, compassion, and courage are the three
> universally recognized moral qualities of men.

References

Chapter epigraphs: www.azquotes.com

CHAPTER 1

Brancati, Frederick. "The Art of Pimping." *Journal of the American Medical Association* 262, no. 1, 1989: 89-90. doi:10.1001/jama.1989.03430010101039.

Rothstein, A. "The Case for 'Pimping' in Medical Education," *The New Atlantis, A Journal of Technology and Society*, 2017, http://practicing-medicine.thenewatlantis.com/2017/08/medical-education-and-case-for-pimping.html.

CHAPTER 2

Livermore, David. *Leading with Cultural Intelligence: The Real Secret to Success.* New York: American Management Association, 2015.

Minhas, Priya. "How Not to Be." In *The Good Immigrant: 26 Writers Reflect on America*, edited by Nikesh Shula and Chinese

Suleyman. New York: Little, Brown and Company/The Hachette Group, 2019.

Singh, Pritma, Afshan Bey, and N. D. Gupta. "Dental Health Attitude in Indian Society," *Journal of International Society of Preventive and Community Dentistry* 3, no. 2 (2013): 81–84.

CHAPTER 3

Angelelli, Claudia V. *Medical Interpreting and Cross-Cultural Communication*. Cambridge: Cambridge University Press, 2004.

CHAPTER 4

This chapter was reviewed by Dr. Raghunath Puttaiah of OSHA4DENTAL, an OSHA and HIPAA training office for dentists.

Wang, Lulu, dir. *The Farewell*. 2019; New York, NY: A24. DVD.

"A Patient's Guide to the HIPAA Privacy Rule: When Healthcare Providers May Communicate About You with Your Family, Friends, or Others Involved in Your Care," US Department of Health and Human Services, Office for Civil Rights, accessed March 12, 2019, https://www.hhs.gov/sites/default/files/ocr/privacy/hipaa/understanding/consumers/consumer_ffg.pdf.

Carter, Ann. "To Release or Not to Release: May Noncustodial Parents Obtain a Copy of Their Child's Medical Records?," Coverys Risk Management, April 2016, http://equotemd.com/wp-content/uploads/April-PHY-IE-2016-To-Release-or-Not-to-Release.pdf.

"Emancipation of Minors," Wikipedia, accessed March 12, 2019, https://en.wikipedia.org/wiki/Emancipation_of_minors.

"How Long Do Parents' Legal Obligations to Their Children Continue?," FindLaw, 2019, https://family.findlaw.com/emancipation-of-minors/how-long-do-parents-legal-obligations-to-their-children-continue.html.

HHS.gov, including the following topics:

- Example of a Policy and Procedure for Providing Meaningful Communication with Person with Limited English Proficiency (LEP)

- Family Members and Friends (45 CFR 164.502 (g) and 164.510 (b))

- May a Healthcare Provider Share a Patient's Health Information with an Interpreter to Communicate with the Patient or with the Patient's Family, Friends, or Others Involved in the Patient's Care or Payment for Care? (45 CFR 164.504(e))

"Does the HIPAA Privacy Rule Permit a Doctor to Discuss a Patient's Health Status, Treatment, or Payment Arrangement with the Patient's Family and Friends?," HHS.gov, 2013 (Section 45 CFR 16.5.510(b)), https://www.hhs.gov/hipaa/for-professionals/faq/488/does-hipaa-permit-a-doctor-to-discuss-a-patients-health-status-with-the-patients-family-and-friends/index.html.

"Must a Covered Healthcare Provider Obtain an Individual's Authorization to Use or Disclose Protected Health Information to an Interpreter?," HHS.gov, 2013 (Section 45 CFR 164.501 (b)

(2) and 45 CFR 164.510 (b)), https://www.hhs.gov/hipaa/for-professionals/faq/760/must-a-covered-provider-obtain-individual-authorization-to-disclose-to-an-interpreter/index.html.

"Personal Representatives," HHS.gov, 2013 (Section 45 CFR 164.502(g)), https://www.hhs.gov/hipaa/for-professionals/privacy/guidance/personal-representatives/index.html.

"HIPAA FAQ," ADA.org, n.d., https://www.ada.org/en/member-center/member-benefits/practice-resources/dental-informatics/electronic-health-records/health-system-reform-resources/hipaa-faq.

"HIPAA Privacy Rule and Sharing Information Related to Mental Health," US Department of Health and Human Services, Office of Civil Rights, accessed March 12, 2019, https://www.hhs.gov/sites/default/files/hipaa-privacy-rule-and-sharing-info-related-to-mental-health.pdf.

Kethcart, Robert. "Emails, Texts, and HIPAA: 7 Rules Every Dentist Needs to Know." *DentistryIQ*, June 29, 2017.

Krager, Dan, and Carole Krager. *HIPAA for Healthcare Professionals*, second ed. Independence, KY: Cengage Learning, 2018.

Stanger, Kim. "Producing Patient Records Upon Request." *AAOMS Today* 17, no. 6 (November/December 2019): 45.

"The HIPAA Privacy Rule," HHS.gov, accessed October 31, 2019, https://www.hhs.gov/hipaa/for-professionals/privacy/index.html.

"Ex-UCLA Healthcare Employee Pleads Guilty to Four Counts of Illegally Peeking at Patient Records," US Attorney's Office, Federal Bureau of Investigation, accessed January 11, 2020, https://

archives.fbi.gov/archives/losangeles/press-releases/2010/la010810a. htm.

CHAPTER 5

Livermore, David. *Leading with Cultural Intelligence: The Real Secret to Success.* New York: American Management Association, 2015.

CHAPTER 6

"Acculturation," *Merriam-Webster*, accessed December 2, 2019, https://www.merriam-webster.com/dictionary/acculturation.

Colby, Sandra L., and Jennifer M. Ortman. "Projection of the Size and Composition of the US Population: 2014 to 2060," United States Census Bureau, March 2015, https://www.census. gov/content/dam/Census/library/publications/2015/demo/ p25-1143.pdf.

"Census Report: More than 20 percent of US Residents Speak a Language Other Than English at Home," LanguageLine Solutions, September 20, 2017, https://blog.languageline.com/ limited-english-proficient-census.

Kriersz, Anday, Ivan De Luce, and Madison Hoff. "This Map Shows the Most Commonly Spoken Language in Every US State, Excluding English and Spanish," *Business Insider*, accessed Jan 18, 2020, https://www.businessinsider.com/ what-is-the-most-common-language-in-every-state-map-2019-6.

Gabriele, Amanda. "The Origins of the Sushi Burrito, Q&A with the Inventor." *The Manual*, April 1, 2019, https://www. themanual.com/food-and-drink/sushi-burrito-sushiritto/.

McCann, Adam. "Most and Least Diverse States in America," Wallethub, September 17, 2019, https://wallethub.com/edu/most-least-diverse-states-in-america/38262/.

Trevelyan, Edward, Christine Gambino, Thomas Gryn, Luke Larsen, Yesenia Acosta, Elizabeth Grieco, Darryl Harris, and Nathan Walters. "Characteristics of the US Population by Generational Status: 2013," United States Census Bureau, accessed January 11, 2020, https://www.census.gov/library/publications/2016/demo/p23-214.html

CHAPTER 7

Wang, Lulu, dir. *The Farewell*. 2019; New York, NY: A24. DVD.

"Languages Included in the Eighth Schedule of the Indian Constitution," Government of India, Ministry of Home Affairs, Department of Official Language, accessed January 11, 2020, https://rajbhasha.gov.in/en/languages-included-eighth-schedule-indian-constitution.

Livermore, David. *Expand Your Borders: Discover 10 Cultural Clusters*. East Lansing, Michigan: Cultural Intelligence Center, 2013.

CHAPTER 8

"Royal Derby Hospital: Disposable Sterile Hijabs Introduced," *BBC News*, accessed January 11, 2020, https://www.bbc.com/news/uk-england-derbyshire-50810176.

CHAPTER 9

Burgess, DJ, J. Warren, S. Phelan, J. Dovidio, and M. van Ryn. "Stereotype Threat and Health Disparities: What Medical Educators and Future Physicians Need to Know," *The Journal of General Internal Medicine*, suppl 2 (May 2010): S169-77. doi: 10.1007/s11606-009-1221-4.

"Caring for a Jewish Patient: A Guide for Medical Professionals," Jewish Visiting, n.d., https://www.jvisit.org.uk/caring-for-a-jewish-patient-a-guide-for-medical-professionals/.

"Guidelines for Healthcare Providers Interacting with Jehovah's Witnesses and Their Families," Metropolitan Chicago Healthcare Council, n.d., https://www.advocatehealth.com/assets/documents/faith/cgjehovahs_witnesses.pdf.

Steele, C.M., and J. Aronson. "Stereotype and the Intellectual Test through Performance of African Americans." *Journal of Personality and Social Psychology* 69, no. 5 (1995): 797–811.

CHAPTER 10

Hung, C. "You look too young to be a dentist," American Dental Association, New Dentist Now Blog, Jan 27, 2020, https://newdentistblog.ada.org/you-look-too-young-to-be-a-dentist/.

"How Many Dental Schools Are There in the US and Canada?" American Dental Association, 2018–19 Survey of Dental Education – Report 1: Academic Programs, Enrollment, and Graduates (Tables in Excel), accessed December 15, 2019, https://www.ada.org/en/science-research/health-policy-institute/dental-statistics/education.

Katuna, Jamie. "'You're Too Small to Be a Surgeon' and Other Things Women in Medicine Hear," January 3, 2018, https://www.jamiekatuna.com/blogs/2018/1/3/youre-too-small-to-be-a-surgeon-and-other-things-women-in-medicine-hear.

Needham, Stephanie. "The Shifting Paradigm of Dentistry: The Predominance of Women." *Dental Economics*, 2017, https://www.dentaleconomics.com/macro-op-ed/article/16389709/the-shifting-paradigm-of-dentistry-the-predominance-of-women.

"The Majority of US Medical Students Are Women, New Data Show," Association of American Medical Colleges, 2019, https://www.aamc.org/news-insights/press-releases/majority-us-medical-students-are-women-new-data-show.

"2018–2019 Survey of Dental Education—Report 1: Academic Programs, Enrollment, and Graduates," Health Policy Institute, Commission on Dental Accreditation, accessed March 11, 2019, https://www.ada.org/en/science-research/health-policy-institute/dental-statistics/education.

OTHER REFERENCES AND RELATED READINGS:

Angelelli, Claudia V. *Healthcare Interpreting Explained*. Routledge, 2019.

Dayer-Berenson, Linda. *Cultural Competencies for Nurses: Impact on Health and Illness*, 2nd ed. Boston, MA: Jones and Bartlett Learning, 2014.

Earley, P. Christopher, and Soon Ang. *Cultural Intelligences: Individual Interactions across Cultures*. Stanford, CA: Stanford University Press, 2003.

Jimenez, Tomas R. *The Other Side of Assimilation: How Immigrants Are Changing American Life*. Berkeley, CA: University of California Press, 2017.

Kennedy, John F. *A Nation of Immigrants*. New York, NY: HarperCollins, 2008.

Ting-Tooley, Stella, and Leeva C. Chung. *Understanding Intercultural Communication*. Oxford, UK: Oxford University Press, 2005.

Start Pulling Wisdom At Your Practice!

ARE YOU CULTURALLY COMPETENT?
TAKE THE QUIZ!

Visit **http://www.drcathyhung.com**
and subscribe to newsletters to learn more about Pulling Wisdom.

FOLLOW PULLING WISDOM ON SOCIAL MEDIA:

FACEBOOK PullingWisdom
@drcathyhung

TWITTER PullingWisdom
@drcathyhung

INSTAGRAM Pulling Wisdom
@pullingwisdom

LINKEDIN Pulling Wisdom

CONTACT DR. CATHY HUNG AT
INFO@DRCATHYHUNG.COM FOR

Writing for your online or print journals or publications on cultural competency or practice management topics.

Speaking book Dr. Cathy Hung to talk about how to "Pull Wisdom" on your show or to speak to your organization on raising cultural awareness, improving cultural competency, and building team success and development as part of practice management.

Coaching

Are you:

- Experiencing discomfort dealing with cross-cultural communication with your patients and/or your team members?

- Looking to improve your practice profitability by improving your cross-cultural communication skills?

- Experiencing cultural shock as a professional at your workplace?

- Feeling isolated in your working environment due to cultural difference?

- Staying in your comfort zone even if you have lived in the US for a long time?

- Serving a demographic that is unfamiliar and uncomfortable compared to your own?

- Needing help with professional presentations because English is your second language?

- A woman professional seeking advice on how to establish authority in your workplace?

Contact Dr. Hung at **info@drcathyhung.com** to inquire about one-on-one or group coaching for you and your practice.

Printed in the USA
CPSIA information can be obtained
at www.ICGtesting.com
JSHW012032140824
68134JS00033B/3006